VISUAL TIMELINE OF THE
20th Century

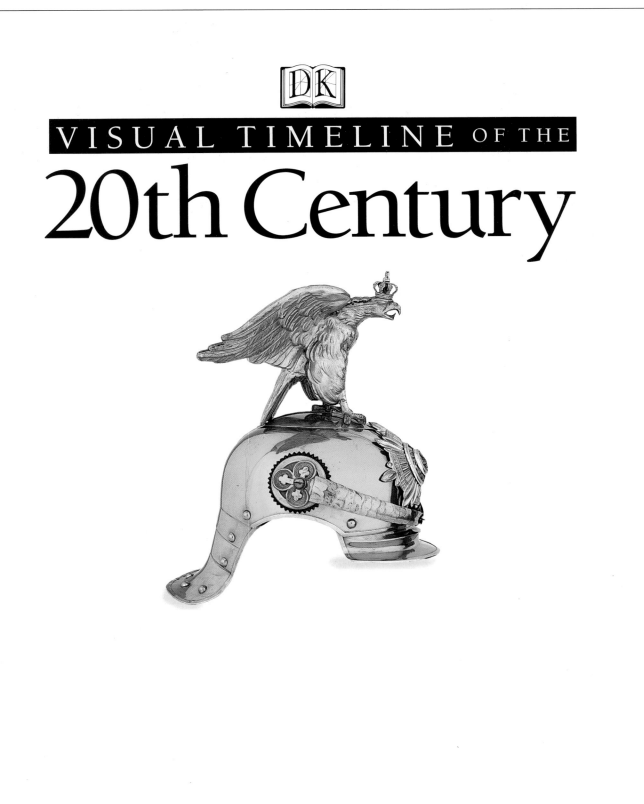

•**1966** *LUNA 9* MOON PROBE

•**1940s** SPOOL OF MOVIE FILM

•**1960s** US PURPLE HEART AWARD

•**1990** MOUNTAIN BIKE

•**1980s** SLR CAMERA

VISUAL TIMELINE OF THE
20th Century

SIMON ADAMS

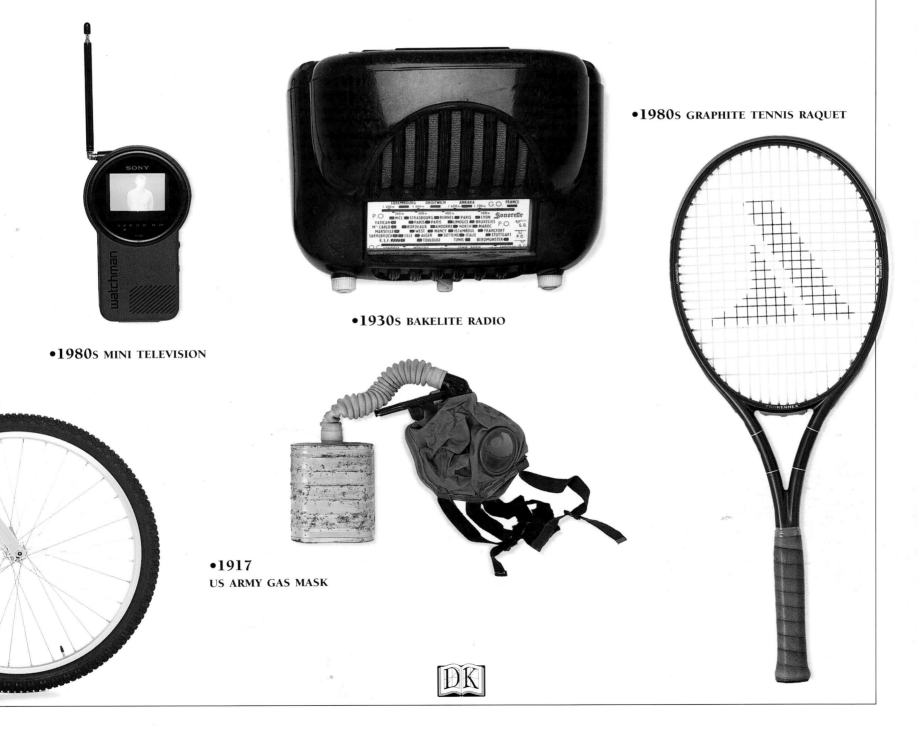

•1980s GRAPHITE TENNIS RAQUET

•1930s BAKELITE RADIO

•1980s MINI TELEVISION

•1917
US ARMY GAS MASK

A DK PUBLISHING BOOK

Project Editor Clint Twist
Art Editor Alexandra Brown
Managing Editor Anna Kruger
Managing Art Editor Peter Bailey
Picture Research Christine Rista
Production Ruth Cobb & Katy Holmes
US Editor Camela Decaire

First American edition, 1996
2 4 6 8 10 9 7 5 3 1

Published in the United States by
DK Publishing Inc.,
95 Madison Avenue,
New York, New York 10016
Visit us on the World Wide Web at http://www.dk.com

A CIP catalog record is available from the Library of Congress.

ISBN 07894-0997-6

Reproduced by Colourscan, Singapore

Printed and bound in Italy by
A. Mondadori Editore, Verona

Contents

Foreword

The 20th century has been a period of rapid and fundamental change, a period in which people's lives have been turned upside down. At the same time as hopes have been raised at the prospects of better health, welfare, and living conditions, those same hopes have been dashed against the reality of two world wars, economic depressions, and potential environmental catastrophe.

Since 1900, life expectancy has risen dramatically due to improved nutrition and better health care, and smallpox and other diseases have been eradicated. New ways of organizing society have been constructed, and new attempts made to solve the age-old problems of poverty and sickness. Literacy levels around the world have also risen, and most children now receive at least a basic education. Many also get the chance to study at the college level and beyond.

Scientist and inventors, through the development of radio, television, and other technologies, have been able to link nations together around the world, send people to the Moon, and launch satellites towards the farthest reaches of our Solar System. Computers have revolutionized every aspect of our lives, and entertainments unthought of even a few years ago are now commonplace in many homes.

Yet this has also been a century of almost continuous warfare. Ten million people died in World War I, and fifty million in World War II – a war in which, for the first time ever, considerably more civilians than soldiers lost their lives. At Hiroshima and Nagasaki, humanity displayed the ability to eradicate all human life from the planet, while in the death camps of Europe, state-organized mass murder was conducted in an attempt to remove one nation from the world for all time.

Perhaps the history of this century will teach future generations that despite the fearful events that may take place, hopes and dreams are still worthwhile. We may eventually learn that the world is too small and too fragile a place for hatred and warfare.

Simon Adams

Simon Adams

1900–1917 The end of an era

Tsar Nicholas II and family: under his rule, Russia slid toward chaos and revolution

THERE WAS NOTHING special about the year 1900. No event singles it out as remarkable in any way. Yet as the years of the new century passed by, it was apparent that the world was changing fast – the old order of the 19th century was drawing to a close. Britain still ruled the seas and controlled the biggest land empire the world had ever seen, but its industrial supremacy was threatened by Germany and, farther afield, by the US. The old empires of Russia, China, Turkey, and Austro-Hungary were declining, and new powers, such as Japan, were taking their place in the world.

The shrinking world

After 1900 the world seemed to shrink: paved roads, railroads, steamships, and telegraphs were already established in many countries. Marconi's radio broadcast across the Atlantic Ocean in 1901 opened up an entirely new method of international communication. A new form of transportation appeared when, after centuries of failure, humankind learned the secret of powered flight, first taking to the skies in 1903. In America Henry Ford developed mass-production, flooding the world with Model T Fords. When the first one was produced in 1908, it took 14 hours to construct; by the end of 1914, each one took just 95 minutes.

Louis Blériot flew across the English Channel in 1909

FLYING MACHINES

After Orville Wright had completed his fourth flight on board the *Flyer* on December 17, 1903, a local newspaper reporter dismissed the historic event with the words: "Fifty-seven seconds, hey? If it had been 57 minutes, then it might have been a news item." The reporter was not alone in doubting the importance of powered flight. As with so many inventions, it took the impetus of war to develop aircraft into sturdy, efficient machines.

Rudder

Fin

Machine gun in observer's cockpit

Tailskid

German identification markings

Aircraft registration code

4503

L.V.G.C.VI 7198/18

THE COUNTDOWN TO WAR: 1900–1917

EMPIRES

A handful of European powers, notably Britain and France, controlled worldwide empires. In Africa only Liberia and Abyssinia retained their independence, while in Asia only Japan and China remained free from European influence. Even the United States acquired overseas territory, in Central America and eastern Asia.

German military helmet with the imperial eagle

Postage stamp from the French colony of Madagascar, 1916

POSTES
10c
MADAGASCAR ET DÉPENDANCES

THE ARMS RACE

Ever since it had become a unified nation in 1871, Germany had worked hard to build up its industrial capacity. Germany also had the strongest army, and, since 1898, had been constructing a navy to rival the British navy, until then ruler of the seas. The rise of Germany prompted the old enemies of Britain, France, and Russia to move closer together, and all European nations began to increase the size and strength of their armed services. By 1914, Europe was an armed camp bristling with weapons.

The first all-steel *Dreadnought*-type battleship was built by Britain in 1906

WARFARE

The war that broke out in Europe in August 1914 was expected to be a short, decisive campaign. Most believed the war would "all be over by Christmas." But the rapid German advance into France was soon halted by the speedy deployment of British and French troops. Both sides dug in for a long war of attrition, which brought appalling casualties – more than 1.5 million troops were killed or wounded in the first four months of the war.

French infantry soldier, 1915

Crowds in central Moscow during the revolution, October 1917

New ideas

Technological change was accompanied by scientific theories that challenged traditional thinking. In Switzerland, Albert Einstein produced two theories of relativity that described how the Universe worked, while the German scientist Alfred Wegener proposed the seemingly ridiculous idea that the world's continents move slowly around the surface of the Earth over many millions of years. Both were subsequently proven right. Just as controversially, the Viennese doctor Sigmund Freud began to explore the human subconscious.

World war

All the rivalries in Europe abruptly came to a head in 1914. When war broke out, few could have foreseen its consequences. Machine guns, tanks, and poison gas transformed the battlefield into a place of mass slaughter. By 1917, it was clear that the old order, dominated by European empires, had ended.

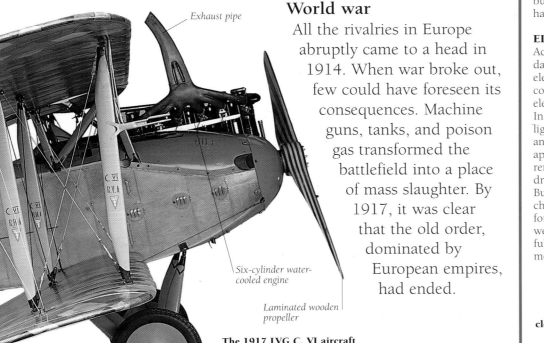

Exhaust pipe

Six-cylinder water-cooled engine

Laminated wooden propeller

The 1917 LVG C. VI aircraft carried a pilot and observer in separate cockpits

DAILY LIFE 1900–1917

Male and female clothing, 1900–1910

CLOTHING

For women of leisure, clothes were extravagant and detailed, and every part of the body from the ears to the feet was covered up. Made of silk, satin, chiffon, or tulle, and decorated with lace or crochet, dresses required a huge amount of time-consuming labor to complete. For those women who worked for a living, cheaper alternatives were available. For men, the accepted wear for all formal occasions was a top hat and frock coat. At more informal times, business suits and homburg (soft felt) hats were worn. Straw hats were also extremely popular.

ELECTRICITY

Across the world electricity was transforming every aspect of daily life. Streets were increasingly lit with electric lights and electric streetcars zipped along. People were able to communicate with each other over huge distances as electricity carried their conversations via the telephone. In the home electric lighting, heaters, stoves, and many other domestic appliances began to remove much of the drudgery of housework. But electricity was not cheap to install or pay for, and only the wealthy obtained the full benefit of this modern invention.

Male and female clothing, 1911–1917

RECRUITING AN ARMY

A sense of patriotic duty filled the armies of both sides with willing recruits in the early months of the war. Many men also joined up to escape unemployment or low pay at home. Those who would not fight were publicly humiliated or attacked as conscientious objectors – in Britain they were sometimes presented with a white feather as a sign of cowardice. But as the war wore on, and the casualties mounted, governments resorted to conscription (compulsory military service) in order to keep their armies up to strength.

Wartime recruiting poster

Women in an armaments factory during World War I

WOMEN AT WAR

As men left to fight the war, women were left to run the country. By 1916, more than 1.6 million women were working in Britain, half of them in engineering plants producing munitions and other supplies. As a result of their efforts, it became increasingly difficult for male politicians to deny women the right to vote and to participate in politics.

Pablo Picasso

THE SHOCK OF THE NEW

The first performance of Igor Stravinsky's music for the ballet *The Rite of Spring* in Paris on May 29, 1913, marked an abrupt break in modern culture. Audiences accustomed to hearing new music that fit in well alongside favorites from the past were appalled at the brutal sounds that assailed their ears. In art, too, the abstract cubist paintings of Picasso and Braque marked a complete break from the realistic style of painting favored up until then. Even literature was affected by this spirit of change, with new writers, such as James Joyce and Marcel Proust, writing daring new novels.

RADIO

The first transatlantic radio broadcast in 1901 marked the start of the radio age. Messages could now be broadcast from continent to continent in seconds. Regular daily broadcasts of entertainment and information began in 1907 in New York, and other cities soon followed.

Marconi radio receiver, c.1900

1900

1900   1901

ARTS & ENTERTAINMENT

Frame indicator

Viewfinder

Film winder

Brownie box camera

•1900 FIRST POPULAR CAMERA

The Brownie box camera, which went on sale in the US for only $1, made photography a popular hobby. Until 1900, photography had been too expensive for most people to afford. US inventor George Eastman eliminated that problem by mass-producing this camera from his factory in Rochester, New York.

•1901 KIM

The British writer Rudyard Kipling won fame for his patriotic stories of the British Empire. However, he is most admired today for his children's books, such as *The Jungle Book* and *Kim*. In 1907 Kipling was awarded the Nobel Prize for literature .

•1901 PABLO PICASSO

Spanish-born artist Pablo Picasso moved to Paris in 1901, where he painted a series of portraits of ordinary working people. Most of the pictures are in blue, and their stark quality marked Picasso as one of the leading young artists of his day.

Teddy bear, c.1903

•1902 TEDDY BEAR

While on a hunting expedition, US President Theodore "Teddy" Roosevelt refused to shoot a bear cub cornered during the hunt. Manufacturers quickly began to produce toy "Teddy's bears." These became an instant and lasting success first in America, and then around the world.

SCIENCE & DISCOVERY

Zeppelin, c.1915

•1900 RIGID AIRSHIP

The German inventor Count Ferdinand von Zeppelin constructed a rigid, aluminum-framed airship kept afloat by lighter-than-air hydrogen. Zeppelins, as these airships soon became known, were fitted with engines that gave them a top speed of about 15 mph (24 km/h).

•1901 TRANSATLANTIC RADIO

Italian-born Guglielmo Marconi sent his first radio communication across a room in 1895. Six years later, Marconi demonstrated the importance of his discovery by transmitting a radio message in Morse Code across the Atlantic, from Poldhu, in Cornwall, Britain, to St. John's, in Newfoundland, Canada.

Guglielmo Marconi

•1902 HORMONES

How the human body grows and develops was a mystery until 1902, when British scientists William Bayliss and E.H. Starling discovered the chemical messengers known as hormones. Carried in the bloodstream, each different hormone is responsible for a different aspect of the body's development.

EVERYDAY LIFE

•1900 ELECTRIC RANGE

Gas ranges were commonplace in kitchens by 1900, but the electric range was very rare because few homes yet had electricity. In order to sell this new appliance, manufacturers emphasized the safety and economy of cooking with electricity rather than with potentially dangerous gas.

Electric range, 1900

•1901 ELECTRIC TRANSPORTATION

Electric streetcars, taking their power from overhead power lines, provided a cleaner, faster, and cheaper alternative to horse-drawn buses. The new electric buses had no need to carry fuel, and did not pollute the streets in the same way that horses did.

•1901 SAFETY RAZOR

King Camp Gillette, a salesman from Wisconsin, developed the safety razor with disposable blades. Within a few years, the era of the old-fashioned straight-edge razor was over.

Model of 1901 electric streetcar

SHEPHERD'S BUSH & KEW BRIDGE.

LONDON UNITED ELECTRIC TRAMWAYS

WORLD EVENTS

•1900 BOXER REBELLION

Angry at foreign interference in China's internal affairs, Chinese nationalists set up a secret organization, the Society of Harmonious Fists, or the Boxers as they were known, to expel all foreigners. An open rebellion by the Boxers in 1900 was put down by European armies that marched into Peking. This foreign intervention greatly weakened the authority of the Chinese government.

•1900 GERMAN NAVAL LAW

Anxious to build a high-seas fleet to rival the powerful British navy, the German government passed a law authorizing the construction of 38 new battleships, thus starting an arms race between Germany and Britain. The new, heavily armed battleships were built entirely of steel and were known as "Dreadnoughts."

Queen Victoria

•1901 QUEEN VICTORIA DIES

Queen of Britain for 63 years and head of an empire that spanned the globe, Queen Victoria died at the age of 82. In her lifetime, Britain had become the world's leading industrial and military power.

•1901 ROOSEVELT PRESIDENT

Following the assassination of President William McKinley, vice-president Theodore Roosevelt became the 26th President of the US. He embarked on a program of industrial and social reform.

•1901 AUSTRALIAN INDEPENDENCE

The six British colonies in Australia agreed to unite and establish a Commonwealth of Australia free from British rule. Social and cultural ties with Britain loosened when Australia became independent.

•1902 BOER WAR

After three years of vicious fighting, the two independent Boer republics in South Africa accepted British control, ending a conflict that had seen the introduction by the British in 1900 of concentration camps.

Boer cavalry

•1902 ANGLO–JAPANESE ALLIANCE

To protect their interests in China, Japan and Britain signed an alliance – the first time that Japan had entered into an agreement with a foreign country.

1903

1903   1904

•1903 JACK LONDON

American writer Jack London wrote *The Call Of The Wild*, about a tame dog that returns to the wild to lead a wolf pack. Based on his own experiences as a gold prospector in the frozen wastes of Alaska, this book is considered one of the best animal stories ever written.

Jack London

•1903 THE WIZARD OF OZ

This new musical opened at New York's Majestic Theater. Based on the 1900 book by Frank Baum, *The Wizard Of Oz* was an instant success. The musical was performed in many countries, and in 1939 it was turned into a successful film.

Illustration from *Peter Pan*

•1904 PETER PAN

The story of Peter Pan, the boy who wouldn't grow up, first appeared as a play by the Scottish dramatist J.M. Barrie. In the story, Peter takes three London children (Wendy, John, and Michael Darling) on a magic trip to Neverland. Together with Peter Pan and the fairy Tinkerbell, the children have many adventures, most excitingly with the pirate Captain Hook. The play rapidly became a popular Christmas pantomime, and in 1911 it was published as an illustrated book. In 1953 *Peter Pan* was turned into a full-length cartoon film by Walt Disney.

•1905 DOUBLE-SIDED RECORDS

By 1905 record players were a feature of many homes, but they were of limited enjoyment because the disks they played were only recorded on one side, and lasted for only two or three minutes. The introduction of double-sided records doubled the length of music available on a single disk, but it was not until the mid-1930s that the 10-in or 12-in record playing at 78 revolutions per minute became standard.

•1903 POWERED FLIGHT

The journey lasted all of 12 seconds, over a distance of less than the wingspan of a jumbo jet, but on December 17, Orville Wright became the first person to fly. The simple gasoline-engined *Flyer*, designed by Orville and his brother Wilbur, took to the air from the beach at Kitty Hawk, North Carolina.

The Flyer was a biplane with two wings linked by vertical struts

Twin propellers powered by a single engine pushed the Flyer slowly through the air

The pilot was supported by a harness slung beneath the lower wing

The Wright brothers' *Flyer*

•1905 TRANSPLANTS

The Austrian surgeon E. Zirm performed the first cornea transplants in 1905, enabling his patients to keep their sight. Since his pioneering operations, cornea transplants and other eye operations have become routine surgical procedures.

•1903 PORCELAIN FILLINGS

The introduction of porcelain fillings meant that dental patients with broken or missing teeth no longer had to pay for expensive metal fillings. Not only were the new porcelain fillings cheaper than gold or mercury amalgam, they also looked more natural.

•1903 GARDEN CITIES

The world's first garden city, a planned suburban ecommunity, was begun at Letchworth, England. The idea for such a city came from Ebenezer Howard, who wanted people to be able to live in the countryside, but with all the benefits of a modern city.

Sigmund Freud

•1904 FREUD

Everybody dreams, but until the Austrian doctor and psychologist Sigmund Freud began to analyze dreams, no serious study of the subject had been made. Freud was very interested in his patient's dreams, and in his 1900 book *The Interpretation of Dreams*, he suggested that dreams express the anxieties and ambitions that people do not recognize while awake. He went on to study and explore other aspects of the human mind, most notably in his 1904 book – *The Psychopathology of Everyday Life*.

•1905 ROTARY CLUBS

American lawyer Paul Percy Harris set up a club of business people in Chicago to promote business cooperation and support local charities. He had little idea that his concept of a Rotary Club – so-called because its meetings rotated between members' places of work – would eventually spread to more than 150 countries.

•1905 ASPIRIN

Use of the new wonder drug, aspirin, spread to Britain and other countries from its birthplace in Germany. Aspirin rapidly became very popular for the relief of headaches and the symptoms of the common cold.

•1903 PANAMA INDEPENDENT

Eager to build a canal between the Atlantic and Pacific oceans through Panama, then part of Colombia, the US government supported a movement that won independence for Panama in 1903. The new Panamanian republic then leased the US a strip of land, and allowed the Americans to begin the construction of a canal.

•1903 ANGLO–FRENCH FRIENDSHIP

The visit of Edward VII of Britain to Paris in May 1903, and the return visit to London of the French president in July, helped build trust between the two countries. This led to the establishment in 1904 of an "Entente Cordiale" (Friendly Agreement) between Britain and France. In 1907 Britain reached a similar agreement with Russia, and the three countries worked increasingly closely together against the threat of German power.

Naval battle, 1905

•1904–05 RUSSO–JAPANESE WAR

Rivalry between Japan and Russia over control of Korea and the Chinese province of Manchuria broke into open warfare when the Japanese attacked the Russian eastern fleet in 1904. Japan then won a series of military victories, finally destroying the Russian Baltic fleet – which had been sent halfway around the world to reinforce the eastern fleet – in May 1905. It was the first time in history that an Asian country had won a naval battle against a European power.

•1905 INDEPENDENCE FOR NORWAY

Part of Denmark until 1814, and then Sweden, Norway finally became an independent nation again after 600 years of foreign rule. The first leader of newly independent Norway was King Haakon VII, a member of the Danish royal family.

•1905 WIDESPREAD UNREST IN RUSSIA

Defeat in the war against Japan, and growing discontent with the harsh rule of Tsar Nicholas II, led to a year of demonstrations and strikes in Russia. In June the crew of the battleship *Potemkin* mutinied, killed the officers, and called for political freedom. Faced with these disturbances, the tsar finally agreed to grant Russia a constitution and set up a parliament (the Duma).

1906

1906   1908

ARTS AND ENTERTAINMENT

•1906 FIRST RADIO PROGRAM

The world's first radio broadcast, a short program containing music and a poem, went on the air in Massachusetts on Christmas Eve, 1906. The first regular daily broadcasts took place the following year in New York.

•1906 JUKEBOX

The John Gabel Automatic Entertainer – the world's first jukebox – played a selection of 24 pieces of music through a large horn. The music was recorded on cylinders, each piece lasting between two and four minutes.

Jukebox, c.1908

•1907 BROOKLANDS RACE TRACK

1906 saw the first Grand Prix at Le Mans, France, which was won by the Hungarian driver Ferenz Szisz, driving a Renault. A year later the world's first race track opened at Brooklands, southwest of London, England. By the time of the first Indianapolis 500 car race in May 1911, motor racing was well established as a major spectator sport.

The Olympic symbol

•1908 OLYMPIC GAMES

The ancient Olympic Games had been revived in Athens in 1896, but subsequent games, in Paris in 1900 and St. Louis in 1904, had been poorly attended. London hosted the games in 1908, and competitors participated in 21 different sports, including, for the first time, the winter sport of ice skating.

SCIENCE AND DISCOVERY

•1906 ALLERGY

Clemens von Parquet, an Austrian pediatrician, first used the term "allergy" to describe the intense, sometimes fatal, reaction some people have to substances that have no effect on other people.

•1906 HYDROFOIL

Working on the principle that wings can lift an object on water as well in air, Italian designer Enrico Forlanni designed a boat raised up on foils. The world's first hydrofoil cruised across Lake Maggiore, Italy, at 38 knots.

Wire connects geiger counter to a source of electricity

Copper cylinder contains low-pressure gas energized by an electrical voltage

Early Geiger counter

•1908 GEIGER COUNTER

Without an instrument to measure radioactivity, no one had any idea how much nuclear radiation a substance gave off. German physicist Hans Geiger devised a counter, which converted the radiation into audible clicks that were counted automatically. The higher the number of clicks, the higher the level of radiation.

EVERYDAY LIFE

•1906 CORN FLAKES

Cooks at an American sanatorium accidentally left some boiled grain unattended, and found it had broken up into crispy flakes. Food manufacturer W.K. Kellogg used this mistake to create a new breakfast cereal called toasted corn flakes.

•1906 COCAINE IN COCA-COLA

After threats of legal action, the Coca-Cola Company of Atlanta, Georgia, replaced the drug cocaine in its drink with caffeine, the stimulant found in tea and coffee.

•1907 BOY SCOUTS

In July, 20 boys spent a few days camping on an island off southern England, learning outdoor skills. The camp was an experiment by Sir Robert Baden-Powell. He was so encouraged by its success that he formed the Boy Scout organization, which now has members all over the world.

One of the first Boy Scouts

•1908 WOMEN'S FASHION

Well-to-do European and American women of this period wore clothing that left only their faces and hands showing. Long skirts covered the legs, tight corsets restricted the waist, and padding emphasized the shoulders. Necklines came high up the throat, while hair was piled up on the head and never worn down.

WORLD EVENTS

•1906 SAN FRANCISCO EARTHQUAKE

A 30-second earthquake destroyed much of San Francisco, California, killing more than 1,000 people and wrecking thousands of homes, offices, and public buildings. The quake caused a firestorm that burned much of the city center to ashes.

•1906 MUSLIM LEAGUE

The campaign against British rule in India was led by an organization called the Indian National Congress. Although the Congress was open to all faiths, many Muslims accused it of favoring Hindus. As a result, the Muslim League was set up to protect the rights of Indian Muslims.

•1906 DREYFUS CLEARED

Eleven years after he was convicted of treason and spying, French Jewish army captain Alfred Dreyfus was cleared of all charges and returned to the French army. At the time, the Dreyfus case had bitterly divided France, with supporters of Dreyfus accusing the army and government of anti-Semitism.

San Francisco after the earthquake and fire

•1907 NEW ZEALAND INDEPENDENT

In September New Zealand joined Australia and Canada as a self-governing dominion within the British Empire: New Zealand had been a British colony since 1840 and had governed itself since 1852.

•1908 BALKANS

Under Austrian control since 1878, the Turkish province of Bosnia-Herzegovina was formally taken over by Austria in 1908. Orthodox Christian Serbs resident in Bosnia resented rule by Roman Catholic Austro-Hungary, and turned to neighboring Serbia for help. Serbia threatened war against Austria, and nearly caused a major European conflict. The crisis was eventually settled in 1909, but Bosnian Serbs continued a campaign of terrorism that ultimately led to a world war in 1914.

•1908 THE CONGO

During the 1880s European countries occupied and claimed most of the continent of Africa. Since 1885 a vast tract of central Africa, called the Congo, had been governed by the Belgian king Leopold II, who had been the principle shareholder in a trading company active in the area. Atrocities against local people in 1903–04 resulted in an international protest against Leopold, forcing him to hand the country over to the Belgian government. Belgium therefore acquired a colony – its only one – that was 80 times the size of Belgium.

1909

•1909 BALLETS RUSSES

With fast-paced choreography and bold, exotic sets and costumes, the Ballets Russes (Russian Ballet) revolutionized modern dance. The company, which held its first season in Paris in 1909, was led by Sèrge Diaghilev. The most famous dancers were Vaslav Nijinsky and Anna Pavlova.

Ballets Russes costume designed by Leon Bakst

The Keystone Cops

•1911 HOLLYWOOD STUDIOS

The first studio to be built in the Los Angeles suburb of Hollywood was established by the Nestor Film Company in October. Other film companies soon followed, including the Keystone Picture Company, established on July 4, 1912, by Mack Sennett, best known for its series of Keystone Cop comedy films. Within a few years, Hollywood was the center of the American film industry.

•1911 MONA LISA STOLEN

The world-famous portrait of the *Mona Lisa* by Leonardo da Vinci was stolen from the Louvre Museum, Paris, on August 21. The painting was eventually recovered in a hotel room in Florence, Italy, in December 1913.

•1909 BLÉRIOT'S FLIGHT

French aviator Louis Blériot was the first person to fly across the English Channel between England and France. He made the historic flight in just 43 minutes.

Blériot sat in an open cockpit

Blériot Type XI monoplane

Frame made from strong wood, such as hickory and ash

Three-cylinder motorcycle engine

•1911 CLOUD CHAMBER

The cloud chamber, for detecting subatomic particles, was devised by C.T.R. Wilson. The chamber contained supersaturated water vapor. As particles passed through the chamber, the vapor condensed around them, leaving a visible trail of tiny water droplets.

Cloud chamber

•1911 ELECTRIC IGNITION

All cars had to be started by hand – by turning a large crank handle – until 1911, when the US car firm Cadillac introduced an electric starter on all its new cars.

•1909 BAKELITE

The first plastic, celluloid, was invented in 1859, but it was suitable only for piano keys and billiard balls. In 1909 the Belgian-American chemist Dr. Leo Baekeland developed a new plastic that he called Bakelite. It was a powder that set hard when heated and subjected to pressure. Bakelite did not burn or conduct heat, and so was ideal for use in electrical equipment.

Bakelite telephone, 1920s

•1910 FOOD MIXER

Labor-saving electric stirrers had been in use in American milkshake parlors since 1904, where they were used to whisk up ice cream and milk into drinks. In 1910 the manufacturers George Schmidt and Fred Osius of Wisconsin produced an electric egg whisk for use in the domestic kitchen.

Advertisement for the ill-fated *Titanic*

•1911 TITANIC

Ocean liners capable of carrying more than 2,000 passengers, and powerful enough to cross the North Atlantic within 5 days, offered affordable travel to a wide range of people. The world's biggest liner, the *Titanic*, was launched in Belfast in May 1911. Disaster struck on its maiden voyage in April 1912, when it hit an iceberg and sank with the loss of 1,500 people.

•1909 TO THE NORTH POLE

On his sixth attempt, American explorer Commander Robert Peary finally reached the North Pole on April 6, 1909. Accompanied by his assistant, Matthew Henson, and four unnamed Inuit, Peary took 36 days to trek across the ice. Although Peary was subsequently honored as the first person to reach the North Pole, his claim was always challenged by Frederick Cook, a surgeon on Peary's first polar expedition.

Robert Peary

•1910 SOUTH AFRICA

Eight years after the British victory in the Boer War, the former Boer republics of Transvaal and the Orange Free State and the British colonies of Cape Province and Natal joined together as South Africa – an independent dominion within the British Empire.

•1910 PORTUGAL

Years of resentment against royal extravagance and the rule of the Catholic Church led to a revolution in Portugal. A three-day rising by workers and members of the armed services overthrew the Portuguese monarchy and set up a republican government.

Pancho Villa (center), famous Mexican revolutionary, 1915

•1911 MEXICAN REVOLUTION

President of Mexico for 45 years, Porfirio Díaz resigned after widespread opposition to his dictatorial rule. Revolution and civil war raged until a new constitution was agreed on in 1917.

•1911 LAST CHINESE EMPEROR

After more than 2,000 years of rule by a series of emperors, China became a republic when a revolt led by the Kuomintang Party of Sun Yat-sen overthrew the five-year-old Chinese emperor Pu Yi.

•1911 TO THE SOUTH POLE

Norwegian explorer Roald Amundsen became the first person to reach the South Pole on December 14, beating a British expedition led by Captain Robert Scott by one month.

1912

| 1912 | 1913 | 1914 |

ARTS AND ENTERTAINMENT

•1912
W.C. HANDY
American bandleader and composer W.C. Handy was one of the first musicians to write down the blues songs previously passed on by word of mouth. Among his own compositions are *St. Louis Blues* and the renowned *Memphis Blues*, which was first published in 1912.

•1913
FUTURIST SCULPTURE
Futurist artists, such as the Italian poet and writer Marinetti, who wrote a manifesto of Futurism in 1909, worshiped new machines and technology. They believed that a new automobile was more beautiful than a classical sculpture. Futurist art is full of movement and action, and often glorifies war.

•1913
THE RITE OF SPRING
Igor Stravinsky's music for the ballet *The Rite of Spring*, first performed by the Ballets Russes in Paris, brought classical music into the 20th century. Today it is considered one of the most important pieces of music written this century.

•1914 35MM CAMERA
The development of the 35mm camera in 1914 led to a huge increase in the popularity of photography. The new cameras were compact enough to carry in a pocket, and did not require the subject to hold a pose while the photographer took a picture. New types of film also enabled photographers to work without flashbulbs.

•1914 JAMES JOYCE
The Dubliners – stories of everyday life in Dublin – established Irishman James Joyce as one of the most important writers of the 20th century. Later novels, especially *Ulysses* (1922), confirmed him as a major literary talent.

SCIENCE AND DISCOVERY

•1913
STAINLESS STEEL
Steel corrodes and is easily damaged, but adding chromium to steel produced a stainless variety that would not scratch or rust. This discovery was immediately applied in the production of high-quality cutlery, coffee pots, and numerous other household goods.

Stainless steel cutlery

Fold-down windshield

Unique Forms of Continuity in Space by Umberto Boccioni, 1913

The Model T came in "any color you want so long as it's black"

Zipper, 1914

EVERYDAY LIFE

•1912
MODEL T FORD
Model T Fords, (first sold in 1908) were originally manufactured one at a time. The introduction of an assembly line and mass-production techniques after 1912 dramatically stepped up production.

Spare tire

Spoked wheel

Model T Ford, 1912

•1914
ZIPPER
It is difficult today to imagine dressing or undressing without the use of a zipper. Yet this simple device was developed only in 1914, after years of trial and error with hooks and eyes.

WORLD EVENTS

•1912 ULSTER
British government plans to give Home Rule to the whole of Ireland ran into intense opposition in Ulster, in the north of Ireland. Here the majority of the population was Protestant and feared control by Roman Catholics from the south. Civil war in Ireland seemed inevitable, but was averted by the outbreak of war in Europe in 1914.

Louise steams through the Panama Canal, 1913

•1913 PANAMA CANAL
After eight years of work, the Panama Canal, linking the Atlantic and Pacific oceans, was finally completed. The steamship *Louise* was the first ship through the Canal in November 1913. The canal was officially opened in 1914.

•1913 US INDUSTRIAL POWER
The US overtook Germany as the richest nation in the world because its industrial production rose steadily throughout the early years of the 20th century. In 1913 the output of American factories exceeded the total output of France, Britain, and Germany combined.

•1913 BALKAN WARS
As the Turkish Empire continued to collapse, European states began to seize Turkish territory in the Balkans. In 1912 Bulgaria, Serbia, Greece, and Montenegro divided the Turkish province of Macedonia between them. Bulgaria did not accept the arrangement, and in 1913 attacked its former allies, although heavy defeats soon followed. As a result of the war, the new state of Albania was created, and Greece emerged as the most powerful state in the region. Fighting in the Balkans considerably increased tension in Europe.

•1914–18
WORLD WAR I
The assassination of Archduke Ferdinand, heir to the Austro-Hungarian throne, in Sarajevo on June 28, 1914, led to a major crisis. Austria declared war on Serbia on July 28; Russia mobilized its forces to help Serbia, and Germany declared war against Russia on August 1, and against France, on August 3. When German forces invaded Belgium on their way to France on August 4, 1914, Britain declared war against Germany. Turkey joined the war on the German side. Because the European powers had colonies around the world, fighting broke out on every continent.

Life in the trenches

• August – Germans defeat Russians at Tannenberg.
• September – British and French troops stop German advance.
• November – A line of trenches stretches from the North Sea to Switzerland, marking the Western Front.

1915

1915

•1915 WAR LITERATURE

World War I had a huge impact on the writers who had to fight in the trenches. Some of them began by writing about the glory of war, but soon turned to depicting its many horrors. After the war, many antiwar poems and books were published – most notably Erich Remarque's novel *All Quiet on the Western Front* (1929).

•1915 WAR ART

Artists, too, were affected by the war, and produced starkly realistic paintings of the devastation caused by the fighting. Paul Nash's painting *We are making a new world* is typical of the period.

We are making a new world Paul Nash (1918)

Albert Einstein

•1915 EINSTEIN

The publication of the *General Theory of Relativity* by German physicist Albert Einstein revolutionized physics by outlining a complete theory of gravity that explained how the Universe works.

•1915 CONTINENTAL DRIFT

When German scientist Alfred Wegener suggested that the continents move around – the reason why fossil tropical ferns are found in the Antarctic, and why Africa and South America fit together – no one believed him. Only in the last 50 years has his theory been generally accepted.

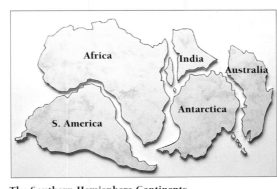

The Southern Hemisphere Continents

•1917 PULITZER PRIZE

In recognition of the growing importance of journalism, the American newspaper publisher Joseph Pulitzer left money to establish a graduate school of journalism at Columbia University, New York. He also funded a series of annual awards for journalism, literature, and music.

•1917 FIRST JAZZ RECORD

The five members of the Original Dixieland Jazz Band, all originally from New Orleans, moved to New York in 1917. There they were so successful that they made a series of recordings for Victor Records – the first jazz records ever made.

•1917 HAHN FINDS PRO-ACTINIUM

Working with a team of colleagues, German scientist Otto Hahn discovered the radioactive element protactinium, a shiny silver-gray metal. For this and other discoveries, notably the splitting of the uranium atom in 1939, he was awarded the Nobel Prize for chemistry in 1944.

•1917 MOUNT WILSON TELESCOPE

The installation of the world's largest telescope – a 100-in (2.5-m) reflecting telescope – at Mount Wilson Observatory in California, enabled astronomers to see much farther into space than ever before.

•1915 WOMEN AT WAR

When men left home to fight in World War I, women were recruited to fill their places in factories, mines, farms, and offices. Many industries previously staffed entirely by men now relied on women to run the production lines. Their success in factories disproved the old idea that women were unsuited to work and were inferior to men, and eventually led to women gaining the right to vote.

•1916 CARING FOR THE WOUNDED

The many thousands of injured soldiers requiring treatment as a result of their wounds led to a number of medical developments. Serum injections were used to treat tetanus caught in the trenches, while plastic surgery became more common for repairing damaged body parts.

V.I. Lenin

One of the first British tanks, 1916

•1916 WORLD WAR I

- February – A major German offensive against the French fort of Verdun lasts for much of the year.
- May – The Battle of Jutland, the only large naval battle of the war, takes place off the coast of Denmark.
- June – More than one million Russians are killed during an unsuccessful attack on Austrian forces.
- July – The Battle of the Somme in France leads to enormous British casualties on the first day of fighting.
- September – Tanks are used by the British for the first time.

•1916 IRISH UPRISING

Angry at the failure of the British to grant Home Rule to Ireland, militant Irish nationalists siezed public buildings in Dublin on Easter Monday and proclaimed a republic. The rebellion was put down with great severity.

•1915 WORLD WAR I

- February – German submarines attack British shipping.
- April – A major offensive by British troops at Ypres, Belgium, leads to major casualties but little ground gained.
- April – Australian, New Zealand, and British forces land in Gallipoli in an attempt to force Turkey out of the war.
- May – The liner *Lusitania* is sunk with the loss of 1,400 lives, including some Americans. The sinking of the liner does much to turn American opinion against Germany.
- June – Russia begins to lose ground against Austrian and German forces on the Eastern Front.

•1917 RUSSIAN REVOLUTION

The failure of the Russian army in World War I led to the abdication of Tsar Nicholas II in March 1917 and his replacement by a liberal government under Alexander Kerensky. The new government continued to fight Germany and Austria, but widespread discontent led to a second revolution in November led by V.I. Lenin and the Bolshevik Party. The world's first Communist state was formed.

•1917 WORLD WAR I

- April – US enters war on Allied side.
- July–November – A major British offensive at Passchendaele, Belgium, leads to 400,000 casualties.
- December – Germany signs an armistice with Russia.

1918–1941 Between the wars

The world that emerged at the end of World War I was utterly different from what had existed before. An entire generation of young men had been killed in battle, and millions were wounded or maimed for life. Entire empires had been removed from the map, and new nations were struggling to survive. Europe was no longer the dominant region of the world, for both Britain and France were exhausted, and Germany lay in ruins. The US was now the most important economic and military power in the world.

The war dead were buried in countless graveyards across Europe

New ideas

The capitalist system of private ownership, practiced in the US, Britain, and France, fell under threat. The Russian Revolution of 1917 led to the establishment of the world's first Communist state. Communists preached common ownership of the means of production, including both land and industry. Many people believed that Communism would offer a solution to the problems of unemployment and poverty. In Europe, many more fell under the power of Fascism, which believed in national domination by a strong government led by a single ruler. Italy in the 1920s, and Germany, Spain, and many nations in eastern Europe in the 1930s, all fell under the power of Fascist dictators.

Automobiles gave people a new freedom to travel

THE MOTOR AGE

As mass production took hold in the American motor industry, car prices fell. By 1930, American Henry Ford had sold 15 million Model Ts, while Volkswagens and Austins had become popular in Europe. Style and performance, however, were restricted to more expensive cars.

Folding windshield for rear passengers

Whitewall tires were a sign of luxury

High-quality paintwork

CONFLICT AND CHANGE: 1918–1941

The Czech-designed Bren light machine gun was used by the British army during World War II

JAZZ AGE

Supported by a booming economy and plenty of money to spend, young people celebrated the Roaring Twenties in style. New dances and new music, notably jazz, were all the rage as bright young things scandalized the older generation with their youthful exploits. The introduction of electrical amplifiers for home use made the new music sound even louder.

CONFLICT

When World War I ended in 1918, people fervently hoped that it was "the war to end all wars." Politicians promised them "a land fit for heroes to live in" and an international organization – the League of Nations – was set up to maintain world peace. Such hopes were dashed when major wars erupted in China, Abyssinia (Ethiopia), and Spain, which the League was powerless to prevent. By the late 1930s it had become clear that the Great War, as World War I was known at the time, was destined to be only the first world war of the twentieth century.

Electric amplifier fitted with valves, 1925

DICTATORS

Economic decline and high unemployment led to a collapse of democracy throughout Europe. Mussolini in Italy, Hitler in Germany, and Franco in Spain all took dictatorial powers to run their countries, while Russia came under the tyrannical rule of Stalin.

German major-general, mechanized infantry regiment, 1939-45

Travel comfortably **IMPERIAL AIRWAYS**
Europe—Africa—India—China—Australia

Lure of the skies

AIR TRAVEL

As aircraft technology became more sophisticated, regular passenger services opened up between most major cities of the world. Air travel might have been slow and uncomfortable compared with today's speedy service, but to a world accustomed to travel by slow train or steamer, it opened up exciting new horizons of travel and adventure.

Paperbacks brought books within the reach of most working people

The Great Depression

The collapse of the New York Stock Exchange in October 1929 and the loss of world economic confidence over the next few years led to an economic and political crisis across the world. Within a couple of years the world's economy had shrunk by almost half. The election of US president F.D. Roosevelt in 1932 led to active intervention in the economy to promote stability and encourage jobs, but most governments preferred to tackle the problem with more orthodox economic measures. As unemployment lines lengthened across Europe and social unrest grew, Adolf Hitler and his Nazi Party took power in Germany in 1933, with a program of rearmament and German territorial expansion in Europe.

The road to war

The direct result of the Nazi Party's program was the outbreak of war in Europe in 1939. At first, Germany and her ally Italy swept all before them. France was defeated, and Britain alone stood up against Germany. But in 1941 the war changed character completely when Russia and the US joined in the fray.

Chromed exhaust pipes

Duesenberg SJ, 1935

DAILY LIFE 1918–1941

CLOTHING

The period between the wars saw a marked change in clothing styles. Women wore simpler, shorter dresses, with hemlines daringly above the knee, and cut their hair short in bobs.

Men, too, wore simpler clothes, with the business suit replacing the frock coat. Bags – very wide-legged pants – were popular, as were knickers, which stopped at the knee. For both men and women, informality and simplicity dominated fashion in this period.

Male and female clothing, 1920s

PROSPERITY AND POVERTY

For most people, daily life in the 1920s and 1930s was a bit of a roller-coaster. Because the US emerged from World War I economically strong, its people enjoyed a wave of prosperity during the 1920s. New electrical goods flooded the market and cheaper cars came within the reach of most families. But European nations were slower to recover from the war. The Depression of the 1930s caused untold misery, with millions unemployed and poverty a fact of daily life. But for those with jobs, the 1930s were a time of falling prices and rising wages. New industries made consumer goods for those with the money to buy them.

Male and female clothing, 1930s

ATOMIC FISSION

After Ernest Rutherford had demonstrated in 1919 that it was possible to split the atom, scientists began work on harnessing the energy produced by the process. The process of nuclear fission – splitting the nucleus of an atom – was discovered by Otto Hahn and Fritz Strassmann in 1938. Their discovery opened the way for both atomic energy and atomic bombs.

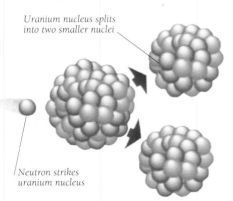

Uranium nucleus splits into two smaller nuclei

Neutron strikes uranium nucleus

Emma Goldman

A NEW ROLE FOR WOMEN

The social upheavals caused by the war promised women liberation from their traditionally subservient roles. Women were among the leaders of revolutions in Ireland, Germany, and Russia, and played an increasingly important political role elsewhere in the world. The American anarchist Emma Goldman lived in Russia for two years, but left in 1921 as the gains of the 1917 revolution were slowly reversed.

THE MOVIES

A whole new industry and way of life grew up around the rapidly expanding American film industry. The silent, and later talking, films threw up a galaxy of film stars, while the studios employed thousands of technicians, screenwriters, producers, and directors. For the public, the movies offered an escape from the routines of daily life, and millions flocked to the cinema every week.

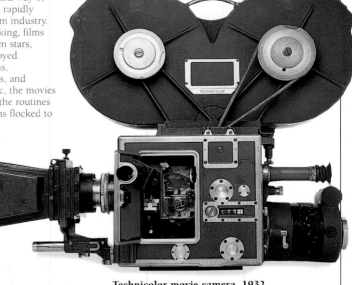

Technicolor movie camera, 1932

1918

Bauhaus building

Charlie Chaplin

ARTS AND ENTERTAINMENT

•1918 HOLST'S *PLANETS*
Written in seven parts, one for each planet (there is no music for Earth, and Pluto was not discovered until 1930), Gustav Holst's *The Planets* was first performed in 1918. It soon became one of the most popular pieces of classical music.

•1918 FIRST TARZAN FILM
Based on the best-selling 1912 book by Edgar Rice Burroughs, the film *Tarzan of the Apes* was released in April 1918, with a sequel, *The Romance of Tarzan*, released the following October. Both films starred Elmo Lincoln. Five more actors played Tarzan in later films, including, most famously, Johnny Weismuller, an Olympic swimming champion.

•1919 CHAPLIN FOUNDS UNITED ARTISTS
Fed up with their acting and directing talents enriching producers, distributors, and film companies, four great Hollywood names – Charlie Chaplin, Mary Pickford, Douglas Fairbanks, and D.W. Griffith – set up the United Artists Corporation to handle their own films.

•1919 BAUHAUS FOUNDED
The Bauhaus school of architecture, design, and crafts, founded in Weimar, Germany, by the architect Walter Gropius, had a huge impact on modern design. Among its teachers were Klee, Kandinsky, and other influential artists who aimed to introduce modern technologies into art and design.

SCIENCE AND DISCOVERY

•1918 QUANTUM THEORY
By explaining how subatomic particles, such as electrons and neutrons, absorb and release energy, the German physicist Max Planck laid the groundwork for the revolutionary Quantum Theory of physics. Planck stated that subatomic particles absorb and release energy in basic units called quanta, not in continuous fashion as previously thought. Planck was awarded the Nobel Prize for physics in 1918.

Atomic nucleus made up of smaller particles

Electrons orbiting the nucleus

Drawing of a carbon atom

•1919 ATOM SPLIT
New Zealand-born physicist Ernest Rutherford was among the first to realize that the atom was not solid, but rather consisted of a single, central nucleus surrounded by orbiting electrons. In 1919 he became the first person to artificially split the atom, thus proving that the atomic nucleus itself was made up of a number of smaller particles.

•1920 DISTANT ASTEROID
Over the centuries, astronomers had identified thousands of pieces of rock known as asteroids orbiting the Sun in a wide belt between Mars and Jupiter. In 1920 the German astronomer Walter Baade identified a single asteroid, which he named Hidalgo, orbiting beyond the planet Jupiter. In 1977 astronomers discovered an even more distant asteroid, which was named Chiron, orbiting the Sun beyond the planet Saturn.

EVERYDAY LIFE

•1918 BRITISH WOMEN VOTE
The first country to give women the vote was New Zealand, in 1893, but it was not until 1913 that the first European women (in Norway) got the vote. After a lengthy campaign, women over 30 could vote in the UK in 1918. In the US, women were allowed to vote for the first time in the elections of 1920.

•1918 "SPANISH FLU" EPIDEMIC
A deadly form of influenza, known as "Spanish flu," swept Europe and America in 1918–19. At least 20 million people died – twice as many as were killed by the fighting in World War I.

Women marching for the right to vote

Hair dryer, 1920

•1920 HAIR DRYER
Handheld hair dryers were first sold by the Racine Universal Motor Company of the US in 1920. They replaced salon-style box dryers, which stood on a table.

•1920 PROHIBITION
The antialcohol movement in America had developed during the 19th century. Total prohibition of alcohol was imposed in the US on January 16, 1920. This led to a thriving trade in bootlegging (the manufacture and distribution of illegal alcohol).

WORLD EVENTS

•1919 HUMAN COST
The best estimate is that more than 10 million died in World War I, while twice that number were wounded. An entire generation of young men was wiped out – a "lost generation" that was never replaced.

•1919 PEACE TERMS
The peace settlement negotiated at Versailles, France, between the Allies and Germany was extremely harsh. Germany had to: surrender all its colonies and some land in Europe; limit its army to 100,000 men with no modern weapons; and pay reparations to those countries its armies had devastated during the war.

War graves in France

Mohandas Gandhi

•1918 WORLD WAR I
The arrival of fresh American troops in Western Europe during 1918, and a successful offensive by Allied troops, led to increasing war-weariness among the German people. The German fleet mutinied at Kiel in October, and both Turkey and Austro-Hungary asked for peace. In November, an armistice was signed between the Allied Powers and Germany, ending the war at the eleventh hour of the eleventh day of the eleventh month.

•1920 GANDHI
After a massacre of protesters at Amristar, northern India, the Congress Party, led by Mohandas Gandhi, adopted a policy of nonviolent disobedience to force the British to leave India.

•1920 LEAGUE OF NATIONS
President Wilson of the US was anxious to avoid future wars by setting up an international organization capable of settling disputes by negotiation. The League met in Geneva, but was fatally weakened by the refusal of the US Congress to join. Although it settled minor disputes, it failed to prevent the Italian invasion of Ethiopia in 1935.

•1920 RUSSIAN CIVIL WAR
Following the revolution of 1917, the Bolsheviks (communists) took power in Russia's big cities, but held little power in the rest of the country. Civil war broke out between the new government and counter-revolutionary opponents known as White Russians, who were aided by European forces. Under the leadership of Leon Trotsky, a communist Red Army repelled the foreign forces and brought the civil war to an end during 1920.

1921

T.S. Eliot

•1922 WASTE LAND

The Waste Land, written by the Anglo-American poet T.S. Eliot, was an immediate critical success when it was published. This lengthy poem describes the barrenness of modern life and the isolation that many people feel. It is considered one of the most important poems of the 20th century.

•1923 COTTON CLUB OPENS

Harlem, a residential section of upper New York, became a center of black culture when large numbers of African-Americans settled in the city. Writers such as Langston Hughes popularized African-American literature, while jazz music flourished in the many clubs in the area. The Cotton Club, in particular, played host to many famous musicians, including Duke Ellington and Cab Calloway.

•1921 INSULIN

The use of the hormone insulin, taken from the pancreas of pigs, offered diabetes sufferers a treatment for their debilitating illness. The discovery was made by two Canadian biochemists, Frederick Banting and Charles Best, and enabled diabetics to inject themselves with the hormone on a regular basis. A synthetic form of insulin was produced in 1966.

Bottle containing pig insulin

•1922 TUTANKHAMEN

In southern Egypt the British archaeologist Howard Carter, sponsored by the Earl of Carnarvon, stumbled upon the untouched tomb of Tutankhamen, the boy pharaoh who died in about 1320 BC. The extraordinary wealth of objects gave historians a new insight into life in ancient Egypt.

Gold mask of Tutankhamen

•1923 ANDROMEDA GALAXY

By studying the Andromeda galaxy in great detail, American astronomer Edwin Hubble proved the existence of other galaxies in the Universe.

•1921 LONDON TO PARIS FLIGHTS

The first public air service began in February 1919, flying between the cities of Berlin and Weimar in Germany. In the same month the first scheduled flights between London and Paris took place, but these were restricted to military personnel because of a continuing wartime ban on international civilian flights. A full civilian service began in 1921 – the first international scheduled passenger service in the world.

•1921 DESIGNER PERFUME

On May 5, French fashion designer Coco Chanel branched out and launched a range of women's perfumes. They are now among the most famous scents in the world.

Chanel, 1921

N°5 CHANEL

•1922 READER'S DIGEST

February 1922 saw the first issue of a new monthly magazine, *The Reader's Digest*. It contained "articles from leading magazines, each article of enduring value and interest in condensed and compact form."

•1922 TELEPHONE SERVICE

By 1922 more than one million people in Britain had a telephone. In the rest of Europe and America many millions more were connected.

•1923 FLAPPERS

In 1922 the American magazine *Vanity Fair* described a new type of young woman, the "flapper." She wore a shapeless short dress, bobbed her hair, and smoked. Flappers hit the headlines the following year when the Charleston dance became all the rage.

A "flapper" dancing the Charleston

•1921 POST-WAR SLUMP

The wartime boom in manufacturing came to an end in 1918. By 1921 most of the European economies were in depression. In Britain unemployment rose to more than one million for the first time since before the war.

Benito Mussolini

•1922 MUSSOLINI IN POWER

Although Italy had fought on the winning side, the war left Italy seriously weakened. Riots broke out in the major cities, and street warfare erupted between communist and fascist gangs. King Victor Emmanuel II called on the fascist leader Benito Mussolini to lead a new government. He quickly assumed dictatorial powers and began an aggressive policy of colonial expansion.

•1922 IRISH FREE STATE FOUNDED

After the war, the British government faced a large Irish republican party – Sinn Fein – demanding full independence from Britain. The British attempted to subdue Ireland by force, but in 1920 agreed to divide the island, granting self-government to the six Protestant countries in the north in 1921. The following year, further negotiations led to the rest of Ireland becoming an independent Irish Free State within the British Empire.

1923 German bank note

•1923 GERMAN HYPERINFLATION

Following its defeat in the war, Germany faced financial collapse as a result of the huge reparations bill owed to the Allies. Inflation increased alarmingly, and by November 1923, a loaf of bread cost 200 billion marks. Economic stability was achieved when a new currency was introduced at the end of 1923.

1924

| 1924 | 1925 | 1926 |

ARTS AND ENTERTAINMENT

•1924 GERSHWIN'S *RHAPSODY IN BLUE*
George Gershwin was the first American composer to combine classical music forms with jazz and folk music. *Rhapsody in Blue*, composed for orchestra, piano, and jazz band, was among his early successes.

•1924 FIRST WINTER OLYMPICS
Winter sports had been a part of the Olympic Games since 1908, but it was not until 1924 that a separate winter event was organized. The first Winter Olympics were held at the resort of Chamonix, in France.

George Gershwin

•1925 LOUIS ARMSTRONG
American jazz trumpeter Louis Armstrong formed the first of his "hot five" bands in November 1925. Over the next five years, he recorded a series of songs that transformed jazz music completely. Until then, jazz was a good-time music played in bars and clubs. Armstrong used simple, popular songs as vehicles for complex improvisation, turning jazz into an art form.

•1925 *THE GREAT GATSBY*
By 1925, America was in the grip of jazz fever as jazz became the most popular music of the day. Author F. Scott Fitzgerald summed up the fast-living, immoral attitude of the time in his novel *The Great Gatsby*, the story of bootlegger Jay Gatsby.

Louis Armstrong

SCIENCE AND DISCOVERY

•1924 FIRST LOUDSPEAKERS
Until the 1920s, music lovers had to make do with sounds that were reproduced mechanically, and radio buffs had to listen in through a set of headphones. The first electrical loudspeakers were produced in the 1920s to overcome these problems, but most of these early designs gave very poor results. The modern electromagnetic loudspeaker was not perfected until 1928.

Early loudspeaker

•1925 EVOLUTION TRIAL
Those who believed the Bible's account of human creation opposed those who believed Darwin's theory of evolution. This debate was argued in an American courtroom in July 1925, after a schoolteacher was prosecuted for teaching Darwin's theory in class. The case itself was fairly unimportant, but the debate still rages.

Baird television, c.1926

•1926 TELEVISION INVENTED
Scottish inventor John Logie Baird demonstrated the first black-and-white mechanical television in 1926. Unfortunately it could not broadcast sound and pictures together, a problem resolved by the development of more successful electronic models in the 1930s.

Black-and-white television screen

•1926 LIQUID-FUELED ROCKET
Powered by a combination of gasoline and liquid oxygen, US scientist Robert Goddard's rocket flew 184 ft (56 m) up into the air, establishing the possibility of space travel.

EVERYDAY LIFE

Large complex aerial to pick up radio waves

Radio receiver, mid-1920s

Tuning controls

•1925 RADIO RECEIVER
Early radio receivers consisted of a crystal of carborundum (a silicon compound) and a fine wire, or "cat's whisker." The wire was twiddled to pick up the radio signals received by the crystal. By 1925, radio sets with valves to amplify the incoming signals rather than crystals and wires (hence "wireless") had become common.

Swastika was Nazi symbol

•1926 FIRST BOOK CLUB
The world's first mail-order book club was formed in the US by Harry Scherman. The Book-of-the-Month Club offered a popular bestseller at a discount price to members of the club through the mail. Book clubs rapidly grew in popularity because few people lived near a bookstore or could afford the prices of new books.

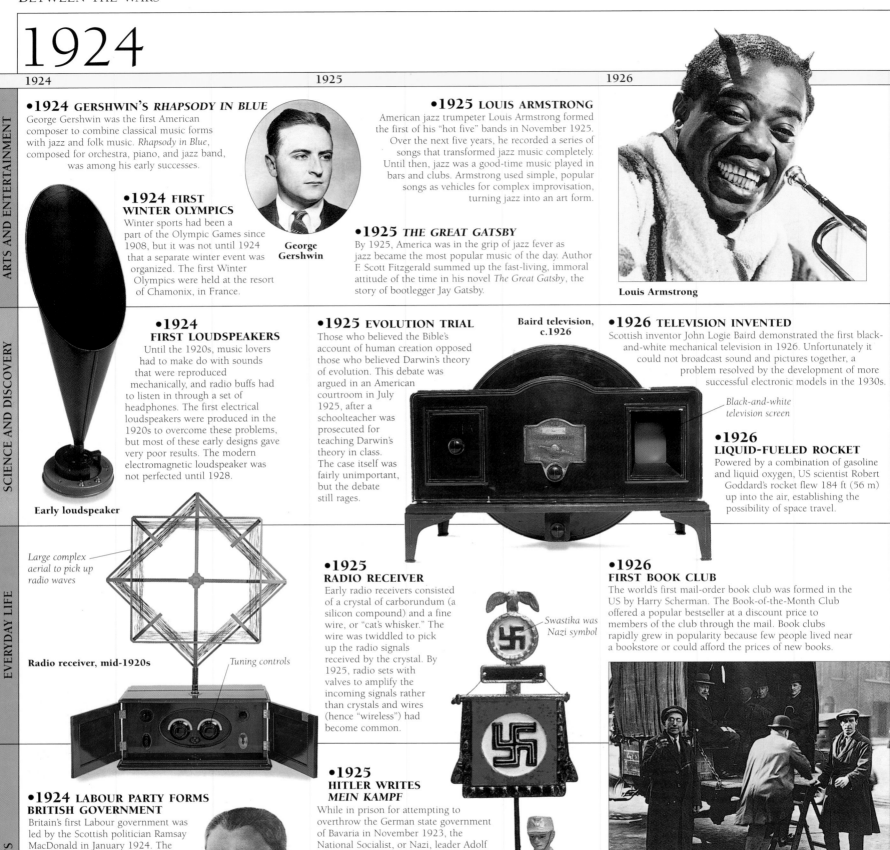

WORLD EVENTS

•1924 LABOUR PARTY FORMS BRITISH GOVERNMENT
Britain's first Labour government was led by the Scottish politician Ramsay MacDonald in January 1924. The Labour Party was founded in 1900 from a coalition of socialist parties and trade unions.

•1924 ATATURK IN POWER
President of the new country of Turkey, which grew out of the post-war remains of the Ottoman Empire, Mustapha Kemal abolished the old religious institution of the Caliphate. He followed a policy of modernizing his country and adopted the title Atatürk – Father of the Turks – in 1935.

Mustapha Kemal Atatürk

•1925 HITLER WRITES *MEIN KAMPF*
While in prison for attempting to overthrow the German state government of Bavaria in November 1923, the National Socialist, or Nazi, leader Adolf Hitler wrote a personal manifesto. *Mein Kampf* (my struggle) outlined a strategy for world domination based on a worship of power and a hatred of Jews.

•1925 LOCARNO PACTS
Seven years after the end of World War I, European nations signed a number of treaties at Locarno, in Switzerland. They confirmed the new borders of Germany, and the demilitarization of the industrial Rhineland region.

Figurine wearing Nazi Party "brownshirt" uniform

Improvised bus transportation during the General Strike

•1926 BRITISH GENERAL STRIKE
In response to moves by mine owners to increase profits by reducing wages and lengthening hours, the miners' unions called for a national strike to resist the moves. "Not a penny off the pay, not a minute on the day," rallied millions of workers to a general strike. The government brought in troops to run essential services, and after nine days most workers returned to work.

1927

•1927 FIRST LAUREL AND HARDY FILM

English-born Stan Laurel (left) and American-born Oliver Hardy made an ideal comedy pair when they starred together for the first time in *Leave Em Laughing*. Over a 20-year period, Laurel and Hardy went on to make some 200 films together.

Stan Laurel and Oliver Hardy

•1928 LADY CHATTERLEY'S LOVER

The novel *Lady Chatterley's Lover*, by English writer D.H. Lawrence, (1885–1930) caused a huge storm because of its explicit sexual content. The book was banned in America and Britain until 1959.

•1928 MICKEY MOUSE

Cartoon character Mickey Mouse made his first appearance on film in Walt Disney's *Plane Crazy*.

•1929 FIRST ACADEMY AWARDS

At the instigation of film producer Louis B. Mayer, the Academy of Motion Pictures Arts and Sciences was set up in 1927 to "raise the cultural, educational, and scientific standards of film." The first Academy awards were handed out in Hollywood on May 16, 1929. The awards became known as Oscars in 1935.

"Oscar" statuette

•1927 FIRST SOLO TRANSATLANTIC FLIGHT

Piloting the *Spirit of St. Louis*, a single-engined monoplane, the 25-year-old American Charles Lindbergh became the first person to fly solo across the Atlantic. He flew from New York to Paris in 33 hours at an average speed of 107.5 mph (173 km/h). His flight took him north to Newfoundland and then east across the ocean. After crossing the Atlantic, Lindbergh flew over Ireland and then southern England before crossing the Channel and flying over northern France. On his return to America, Lindbergh was honored as a hero.

Penicillin culture

•1928 PENICILLIN

The chance discovery of a mold, *Penicillium notatum*, that could kill bacteria led the Scottish biologist Alexander Fleming to develop the drug penicillin. However, because the new drug could only be made in small quantities, it was not immediately identified as an all-powerful antibiotic, able to treat many human illnesses.

•1929 AERIAL ARCHAEOLOGY

Aviator Charles Lindbergh and his wife, Anne, flew over the ancient Pueblo villages of the southwestern US and over the ruins of ancient Mayan temples in Belize, Central America, to investigate the sites from the air. What was unseen from the ground became much clearer from the air as outlines of buildings and walls stood out against the surrounding landscape.

Al Capone (center) after his arrest in 1931

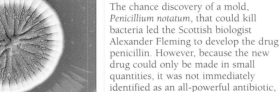

•1927 US GANGSTERS

The introduction of Prohibition in America in 1920 led to a rise in organized crime because gangsters controlled the illegal production and distribution – bootlegging – of liquor and its sale in secret speakeasies (drinking dens). The most famous gangster, Al Capone, terrorized Chicago, controlling the city's drink, gambling, and lottery rackets. It was estimated that he earned $105 million in 1927 alone.

•1927 AIR TRAVEL

Throughout the 1920s, air travel was becoming faster, more efficient, and cheaper. In America, both Pan American and Eastern Airlines were founded in 1927, promising regular flights between major cities. Air France took to the skies in 1933, and the British Overseas Airways Corporation (BOAC), the forerunner of British Airways, first flew in 1939.

•1929 THE "ROARING TWENTIES" END

The decade after World War I was a relatively peaceful period when most world economies grew considerably in size. Most people shared in this wealth and had more money to spend on entertainment and leisure than ever before. Theater, radio, dance halls, and clubs all flourished. The so-called "Roaring Twenties" came to a sudden halt in 1929.

•1927 CHIANG KAI-SHEK

After the death of the Chinese nationalist leader Sun Yat-sen, the struggle to control the Kuomintang party, which ran the government, was won by Chiang Kai-shek. Chiang was an able military leader and by 1927 had consolidated his authority over the army and most of the country, but he was opposed by the Communist Party.

•1927 CANBERRA CAPITAL OF AUSTRALIA

Ever since Australia had become independent from Britain in 1901, the country's capital had been Melbourne, the state capital of Victoria. By 1909 the decision was taken to build a new capital at Canberra, in New South Wales. In 1927 the first meeting of the Australian parliament took place in the city.

Josef Stalin

•1928 STALIN IN CONTROL OF USSR

After the death of Lenin in 1924, a power struggle erupted for control of the Soviet Union between the Red Army leader Leon Trotsky and the Bolshevik party secretary Josef Stalin. By 1928 Stalin was in full control and began to carry out his policy of "Socialism in One Country," taking over state control of all land and starting a program of industrialization.

•1928 SALAZAR TAKES POWER

After the revolution in 1910, Portugal endured years of poor government. In 1928 a young economics professor, Antonio Salazar, became minister of finance. He showed such skill at handling the economy after the slump of 1929 that he was made prime minister in 1932 and given almost dictatorial powers. Salazar ruled Portugal until 1968.

Wall Street in 1929

•1929 WALL STREET CRASH

After years of rising prices, the New York Stock Exchange crashed on October 24, 1929. The fall continued until the end of the month, causing banks and businesses to fail, and millions of people to lose all their savings. Within months, the powerful American economy was in recession. Other countries, especially in western Europe, soon followed the US into an economic slump.

1930

1930

1932

ARTS & ENTERTAINMENT

•1930 PINBALL MACHINE

The pinball machine was invented in Chicago, Illinois, as entertainment for unemployed workers during the Depression years. The advent in 1947 of flippers, used to keep the ball in play, massively improved the enjoyment of the game.

•1930 FIRST WORLD CUP

Confirming soccer as the world's most popular sport, 11 nations, including four from Europe, competed for the first World Cup in Uruguay. The home team won the final match 4–3 against Argentina.

World Cup final, 1930

Electromagnetic pickups transform vibrations of strings into electrical impulses

Early electric guitar

•1932 ELECTRIC GUITAR

The electric guitar evolved through a series of experiments designed to increase the volume of existing acoustic instruments. Swiss-born California-resident Adolph Rickenbacker first amplified a guitar by using electromagnetic pickups on the strings, feeding the sound through an amplifier to a loudspeaker.

SCIENCE & DISCOVERY

•1930 AMY JOHNSON

On April 24, British aviator Amy Johnson touched down in Darwin, on the north coast of Australia, becoming the first woman to fly solo from Britain to Australia. The 10,000-mile flight took 19 days, and made Johnson a role model for women around the world.

Amy Johnson

•1931 ELECTRON MICROSCOPE

The first electron microscope was developed by the German scientist Ernst Ruska. By bombarding specimens with electrons (rather than light) and recording the results on a TV screen, his machine magnified objects 17 times. Within a few years scientists had built models that magnified many times more powerfully.

•1931 VITAMIN A

Throughout the 1920s and 1930s, scientists succeeded in isolating individual vitamins. This allowed them to produce vitamin supplements to help patients with particular vitamin deficiencies. In 1931 Swiss biochemist O.P. Karrer isolated vitamin A, essential for healthy skin.

•1932 NEUTRON DETECTOR

Neutrons, the uncharged particles in the nucleus of an atom, were discovered by James Chadwick in 1932. Before his discovery, it was thought that an atomic nucleus consisted only of the positively charged protons that were discovered by Rutherford in 1919. More recently, scientists have decided that protons and neutrons are themselves made of smaller particles called quarks.

Chadwick's neutron detector

EVERYDAY LIFE

•1930 SPORTS CLOTHES

Sports began to influence fashion in the 1930s when outdoor games became increasingly popular. The simple clothes required for tennis, golf, and other sports were imitated in everyday fashion. Both men and women found the new styles liberating and daring, a reaction against the more restricting clothes they wore for work.

Advertisement for sports clothes

•1931 EMPIRE STATE BUILDING

The world's then tallest building, the Empire State Building in New York, opened on May 1. Towering 1,245 ft (381 m) above Fifth Avenue, the building contains 86 stories of offices and restaurants. Both the World Trade Center in New York and the Sears Tower in Chicago have since surpassed its height, as have several communications towers and masts.

Empire State Building

•1932 WORLD DEPRESSION

The slump caused by the crash of the New York Stock Exchange in October 1929 turned into a worldwide depression as banks failed around the world, withdrawing their finances from industry and commerce. By 1932 international trade had slumped by more than 60%, world industrial production had fallen by 40%, and more than 12 million people were out of work in the US alone, with many millions more unemployed in Europe, South America, and Australasia. Entire industries closed down, and many towns and communities came to a standstill.

WORLD EVENTS

•1930 HAILE SELASSIE

The coronation of Haile Selassie as Emperor of Abyssinia, as Ethiopia was then known, began a period of great reform in the only African nation that was independent of European rule. Attempts were made to modernize the government and to improve health and education.

Haile Selassie

•1930 WORLD POPULATION

In 1930 the world population rose above 2 billion for the first time, rising from 1.834 billion in 1920 to 2.028 billion. More than half this total lived in Asia, with 17.6% in Europe and only 7.7% in Africa. The most populous country was China, with 410 million people.

•1931 SPAIN BECOMES A REPUBLIC

After years of mounting protest against King Alfonso XIII and his dictatorial prime minister Primo de Rivera, republican parties won an overwhelming vote in local elections in early 1931. A republic was declared in December 1931, with Alcalá Zamora as president and Manuel Azaña as prime minister.

•1931 STATUTE OF WESTMINSTER

The British Commonwealth came into being in December 1931 when the British government passed the Statute of Westminster. Canada, Australia, Ireland, and other former colonies were defined as being "equal in status...and freely associated as members of the British Commonwealth of nations."

•1932 F.D. ROOSEVELT ELECTED

Franklin D. Roosevelt became the 32nd president of the United States when he won a landslide victory against the former president Herbert Hoover. Roosevelt, a Democrat, "pledged a new deal for the American people" in tackling the effects of the Depression.

•1932 ZUIDER ZEE SCHEME

The completion of the Zuider Zee drainage scheme in the Netherlands, begun in 1920, converted the huge inlet of the Zuider Zee into an inland lake. Much of the lake was drained and turned into farmland, providing much-needed jobs.

F.D. Roosevelt

1933

1933

•1933 LORCA'S *BLOOD WEDDING*
With the premiere of his play *Blood Wedding*, the Spanish poet Federico García Lorca (1898–1936) established himself as one of Europe's leading dramatists. Lorca was assassinated by nationalist forces at the beginning of the Spanish Civil War in 1936.

•1933 STEREO RECORDING
Until the early 1930s all records were "mono" – they were recorded with a single microphone, and played back through a single loudspeaker. Victor Records began to experiment with stereo sound in 1931–32, but the first stereo records did not go on sale until 1933.

•1933 HEAVY WATER
Discovered in 1932, deuterium, or "heavy hydrogen," is an isotope of hydrogen that has both a proton and a neutron in its nucleus. In 1933, Gilbert Louis managed to produce nearly pure deuterium oxide (also known as "heavy water"), which is now used in some nuclear power stations.

Sample of heavy water

The winning putt, 1934

**•1934
FIRST US MASTERS
COMPETITION**
The first Masters Tournament was held at the Augusta National Golf Club, Georgia, in 1934. Along with the existing British and US opens and the United States Professional Golfers' Association championship, the Masters rapidly took its place as one of the world's four major golf tournaments.

Sample of the first nylon fabric, 1934

•1934 NYLON
While searching for an artificial replacement for silk, W.H. Carothers and his team drew out an elastic thread from plastic. Nylon, as it was called, became a hugely versatile substance that was first used for making toothbrushes. Nylon stockings were first worn in 1940.

Hoover Building

•1935 ART DECO
The Art Deco style took its name from a 1925 exhibition of "arts décoratifs" in Paris. Initially it was associated with interior design, but was later applied to whole buildings, especially theaters and factories. A fine example is the Hoover Building in the west of London, built in 1935.

•1935 RICHTER SCALE
American geophysicist Charles Richter (1900–85) devised an open-ended scale to measure the size or magnitude of an earthquake, replacing an earlier 12-point scale. An earthquake in Chile in 1960 that measured 8.9 on the Richter scale was the biggest quake recorded to this day.

•1935 MAGNETIC TAPE
Magnetic sound recording onto spools of wire was developed in 1898, but was of little practical use because the wire spools were very unreliable. The invention of magnetic tape by the German company I.G. Farben in 1935, and the production soon afterward of the first "Magnetophon," or tape recorder, enabled sound to be recorded and played back with ease.

"Dust Bowl" scene in the American Midwest, 1930s

•1934 DUST BOWL
In the United States, drought and dust storms created a "Dust Bowl" landscape in the Midwest. Thousands of farmers abandoned their farms and headed west to find work in the fruit plantations of California, a journey immortalized by John Steinbeck in his novel *The Grapes of Wrath* (1939).

•1934 ECONOMIC REVIVAL
Unemployment lines started to shorten around the world as industries began to prosper once more. However, rearmament in the face of German military revival was the most significant factor in revitalizing the world economy.

DC3 - "Dakota"

•1935 DC3 AIRCRAFT
The dependable Douglas DC3 (the "Dakota") took its first flight in 1935. Carrying up to 21 passengers at 170 mph (270 km/h), the DC3 soon became the workhorse of the skies, carrying 90% of all airline passengers by 1939. During World War II, Dakotas were used for dropping paratroops as well as for carrying cargo and passengers.

**•1933
HITLER
TAKES POWER IN GERMANY**
In January 1933, Adolf Hitler, leader of the extreme right-wing Nazi party, took power in Germany. At first the Nazis governed with the support of other right-wing parties. In February 1933, Hitler assumed total dictatorial powers. Jews and liberals were persecuted and beaten, and trades unions banned.

**•1933
US NEW DEAL**
Within days of his election as US president, Franklin D. Roosevelt instituted a "New Deal" to get America back to work. New government agencies were established to regulate industry, start up public works programs, and build a huge series of hydroelectric power plants in the Tennessee Valley.

Adolf Hitler, 1933

**•1934
LONG MARCH**
By 1934 the Chinese Communists were losing their struggle against the government. Led by Mao Zedong, 100,000 Communists left their former stronghold in the southeast of the country in October 1934. They marched 6,000 miles (9,700 km) west and then north before settling in Shaanxi Province in the north of the country almost a year later.

**•1934
SOVIET PURGES**
By 1934 Stalin was the undisputed leader of the USSR. Over the next four years, half the generals in the Red Army and many leading politicians were shot, imprisoned, or exiled. Non-Russian minorities were sent to labor camps and millions of Russians were sent to work in Siberia.

Italian troops in Abyssinia

**•1935
ITALY INVADES ABYSSINIA**
Anxious to create an African empire to match that of the British and the French, the Italian government of Mussolini invaded Abyssinia in October 1935. The ill-equipped Abyssinian army was no match for the tanks, planes, and poison gas of the Italian army, and the country surrendered in May 1936.

1936

1936   1937

ARTS AND ENTERTAINMENT

•1936 JESSE OWENS

The star of the 1936 Olympic Games, held in Berlin, was the black American athlete Jesse Owens. He won four gold medals – in the 100 m, 200 m, long jump, and as part of the 100-m relay team – but was snubbed by Adolf Hitler, who refused to acknowledge Owens's achievements when presenting the medals because of his skin color.

Jesse Owens, 1936

•1937 GUERNICA

Commissioned to contribute a painting to the Spanish Pavilion in the 1937 International Exhibition in Paris, Pablo Picasso painted *Guernica*. It was a furious response to the bombing of a Basque village by German planes during the Spanish Civil War.

•1937 SNOW WHITE

After four years in production, Walt Disney's first feature-length cartoon film – *Snow White and the Seven Dwarfs* – premiered in December 1937. The film became an immediate hit with audiences around the world.

•1938 BRIGHTON ROCK

The English novelist and playwright Graham Greene achieved international fame with *Brighton Rock*, a powerful novel about a teenage gangster in Brighton, England, and how he is brought to justice. The novel was later made into a film starring Richard Attenborough as Pinky the gangster.

Electric motor drives paper-carrying rollers

The first photocopier, 1940

SCIENCE AND DISCOVERY

•1936 J.M. KEYNES

In his book *The General Theory of Employment, Interest, and Money*, published in 1936, the British economist John Maynard Keynes became the first person to explain how governments might solve unemployment through public spending.

Air-cooled engine at rear

•1937 JET ENGINE PROTOTYPE

In 1937, British scientist Frank Whittle built a prototype jet engine, which powered its first aircraft in 1941. However, credit for the first jet aircraft flight belongs to the German engineer Hans von Ohain in 1939.

Luggage space under hood

•1938 PHOTOCOPIER

By using static electricity to stick ink particles onto paper, American physicist Chester Carlson invented the world's first photocopier. In 1947 the Haloid Corporation acquired the rights to the invention and gave a public demonstration of a new, reliable machine in 1948.

•1938 BALLPOINT PEN

A Hungarian proofreader, Ladislao Biro, was tired of blotting the pages every time he used his fountain pen to mark errors in text. So he and his chemist brother Georg together developed the first ballpoint pen in Budapest in 1938.

Ballpoint pen, 1938

EVERYDAY LIFE

Volkswagen "Beetle"

•1936 PEOPLE'S CAR

The Volkswagen "Beetle" revolutionized car ownership after the 1930s. In order to increase vehicle-building capacity for the war effort, and also to provide a cheap car for the mass population, the German government of Adolf Hitler supported the development of a "people's car," or Volkswagen. The first prototype Volkswagen Beetle was produced in 1936.

WORLD EVENTS

•1936 SPANISH CIVIL WAR

Opposition to the left-wing policies of the Spanish republican government broke out into open revolt in early 1936 when army forces led by General Franco declared war on the government. The war quickly became an international battleground, with Russia aiding the republicans, and Germany and Italy aiding the rebels. Greater firepower and better organization led to victory for Franco in 1939.

Hindenburg disaster

•1937 HINDENBURG

The German airship *Hindenburg* crashed with the loss of 35 passengers and crew when trying to land in Lakehurst, New Jersey, on May 6 in bad weather. This disaster marked the end of rigid airships as a means of travel, although non-rigid blimps have continued to be used.

•1937 JAPAN INVADES CHINA

Since 1931 Japan had occupied the northern Chinese province of Manchuria. From this base, Japan launched a full-scale invasion of China in July 1937. Japanese forces soon controlled the whole of the coastline, including the Chinese capital of Nanking, and committed atrocities against the civilian population. The invasion forced the two sides in the Chinese civil war – the government of Chiang Kai-shek and the Communists – to join forces in an uneasy alliance against the Japanese.

•1938 GERMANY AND AUSTRIA

On March 13 the Austrian government proclaimed *Anschluss* (political union) with Nazi Germany, despite being forbidden to do so by the 1919 Treaty of Versailles. The union was subsequently ratified by a referendum.

Neville Chamberlain after the Munich Conference

•1938 MUNICH AGREEMENT

In 1938 Germany threatened war over Czechoslovakia. War was averted by a four-power conference at Munich in September, at which German demands were met. The British prime minister Neville Chamberlain stated that Munich promised "peace for our time," although at best it averted the outbreak of war for another year. Germany occupied the rest of Czechoslovakia in March 1939.

1939

•1939 *GONE WITH THE WIND*
Starring Clark Gable as Rhett Butler and Vivien Leigh as Scarlett O'Hara, *Gone With The Wind* premiered on December 14 in Atlanta, Georgia. The film, which lasts for 3 hours 42 mins, is based on the novel by Margaret Mitchell and is an epic tale of love set against the background of the American Civil War.

•1939 *THE HOBBIT*
J.R.R. Tolkein, an Oxford professor of medieval studies, wrote the fantasy story *The Hobbit*, based upon bedtime tales he had made up for his own children.

•1940 *THE GREAT DICTATOR*
Charlie Chaplin's first sound feature film was a hard-hitting attack on Hitler and Mussolini. Chaplin starred as Adenoid Hynkel, the dictator of Tomania – a parody of Adolf Hitler.

•1940 HEMINGWAY
American writer Ernest Hemingway's novel *For Whom The Bell Tolls*, set in the Spanish Civil war, is one of the great war novels of the century. Hemingway was awarded the Nobel Prize for literature in 1954.

***Gone With the Wind* film still**

Orson Welles

•1941 *CITIZEN KANE*
Twenty-five-year-old film director Orson Welles made an extraordinary debut film. *Citizen Kane*, starring Welles in the leading role, concerns a powerful press baron loosely modeled on William Randolph Hearst, one of the most important newspaper owners in the United States.

•1939 DDT   **Aerial spraying, mid-1940s**
DDT, the world's first synthetic insecticide, was developed in 1874, but it was not until 1939 that the Swiss scientist Paul Müller recognized its potential for killing malaria-carrying mosquitoes.

•1940 RADAR/MAGNETRON
The development of radar – Radio Direction And Ranging – grew out of the necessity for British and German forces to detect each other's incoming aircraft during a war. In 1940 two British scientists developed the cavity magnetron, a compact valve that made airborne radar possible. This invention was put to immediate use in World War II, when radar was used to warn pilots of incoming German aircraft, as well as to show bombers their targets in enemy territory.

Copper tubing circulates cooling water around magnetron

Glass tube connects to a vacuum pump

Electrons are whirled around inside a magnetic field to produce a radar beam made up of microwaves

Prototype magnetron

•1939 AIR-RAID PRECAUTIONS AND EVACUATION OF CITIZENS
The declaration of war in Europe in September 1939 affected the entire populations of the combatant countries. In Britain and France, women and children were evacuated from the big cities, and schools relocated to the countryside. Because of the fear of aerial bombing, air-raid shelters were built in most towns, and people were instructed as to how to make their homes safe from bombardment.

Rationing, 1940

•1940 RATIONING
The threat of attacks on shipping meant that imported goods were in short supply across the whole of Europe. Food, fuel, and other necessities were all subject to rationing. Everyone was given a ration book, which allocated a weekly share of food, and people were encouraged to grow their own vegetables.

German army in Paris, 1940

•1939–45 WORLD WAR II
By 1939 the German government of Adolf Hitler had rearmed sufficiently to wage all-out war in pursuit of its goal of European domination and *Lebensraum* (additional territory for the German people). A non-aggression pact was signed with the USSR in August 1939, which allowed Hitler to invade Poland in September 1939 without fear of Russian reprisals. Britain and France declared war on Germany on September 3.

•1940 WORLD WAR II
- April – Germany invades Denmark and Norway, which surrender in May.
- May – Germany invades Holland and Belgium. Winston Churchill becomes British prime minister.
- May – Germany invades France, which surrenders after 7 weeks.
- June – 320,000 British and French troops are evacuated from the French port of Dunkirk.
- June – Italy enters war on German side.
- July – Germany begins bombing attacks on Britain in preparation for a full-scale invasion. Aerial dogfights between British and German pilots during the Battle of Britain gradually turn in Britain's favor as the increased numbers of Spitfire fighter aircraft begin to overwhelm the German bomber forces. By the end of September, Germany abandons its plans to invade Britain, switching instead to an intensive bombing campaign against British cities.
- September – Italian forces invade Egypt.
- October – Italian forces invade Greece, but are driven back.

Pearl Harbor, 1941

•1941 WORLD WAR II
- January – British and Commonwealth forces make progress against the Italians in North Africa.
- April – Germans invade Yugoslavia and Greece.
- June – A huge German army of 320,000 troops invades the USSR, bringing the country into the war on the Allied side.
- September – German army begins 900-day siege of Leningrad.
- October – German army begins assault against Moscow.
- December – Japanese attack US naval fleet at Pearl Harbor in Hawaii. The US declares war on Japan and Germany, turning a European war into a truly world war.
- December – Japanese invade Hong Kong and over next few months conquer most of Southeast Asia.

23

1942–1989 The divided world

Planet Earth, photographed from space during one of the US Moon missions

The entry of both the US and the USSR into World War II turned the European war into a truly international conflict, fought out on every continent. The battles of El Alamein in North Africa, Midway in the Pacific Ocean, and Stalingrad in southern Russia in 1942–43 marked the turning point in a war that was to last until 1945 and cost the lives of more than 50 million people. Entire cities were wiped off the map, and millions of civilians were killed as a result of bombing.

Hawker Harrier GR5, 1989

MILITARY HARDWARE

The political competition between the US and the USSR led to a massive build-up of armaments after 1945. New aircraft, such as the British-designed Harrier jump jet (above), commanded the skies, while aircraft carriers altered the nature of sea warfare because their aircraft could attack targets way beyond the range of any warship's guns.

After the war

Two events distinguished the war as the most brutal conflict in history. The deliberate policy of Nazi Germany of racial genocide against European Jews, known today as the Holocaust, was carried out with such detailed planning and with the involvement of so many different individuals that it revealed to everyone the inhuman lengths people are prepared to go to in pursuit of their goals. The dropping of the two atomic bombs on Japan in August 1945 showed that humankind could now destroy life on a massive scale. Together the Holocaust and the bomb have cast shadows on every aspect of life in the second half of the 20th century.

Radar antenna

Communications mast

Carrier aircraft often have folding wings

A model of the aircraft Carrier HMS Eagle, 1964

A WORLD IN CONFLICT: 1942–1989

THE HOLOCAUST

In 1942, leading Nazis devised the "Final Solution" to the Jewish "problem." Jews, as well as gypsies, Slavs, and other "undesirables," were to be herded together in death camps such as Auschwitz–Birkenau and Treblinka. These camps were in addition to concentration camps, such as Belsen and Dachau, which already provided slave labor for armaments and other industries. Altogether, about 6 million were killed.

The inmates of Dachau camp, following their liberation by Allied troops

In Nazi Germany, Jews were forced to wear a yellow star on their clothing

The UN flag

THE UNITED NATIONS

The pre-war League of Nations had failed to prevent war, and all but collapsed in 1939. In its place the allied nations fighting Germany and Japan set up a more robust organization better able to keep the peace. The United Nations charter was signed in San Francisco on June 26, 1945; the organization met for the first time in London in 1946. The UN has had several successes, notably in the Middle East, but has usually only succeeded when the world's major powers were in agreement.

Weapons, uniform, and equipment of a US infantryman in Vietnam

VIETNAM

Vietnam endured almost constant warfare from 1941, when it was invaded by Japan, through the struggle in the 1950s to free it from French colonial rule, until 1975, when the country was finally unified. The most savage phase of fighting began in 1965, when US ground troops fought the Communist Vietminh army of North Vietnam. The US air force mounted a huge bombing campaign against the north.

Two worlds and more

After the war, the US and the USSR parted ways as mutual distrust of each other's goals led to a cold war between them. By 1949 Europe was divided into two armed camps, and both sides engaged in an arms race that nearly led to nuclear conflict over Cuba in 1962. Conflicts between allies of the two superpowers erupted in Korea and Vietnam. But much of the world chose to turn its back on the rivalry between the US-led First World and the Communist Second World. When the former colonies of Britain, France, and other European nations gained their independence, many of them joined together in a non-aligned movement to press for a fairer deal for the Third World nations of Africa and Asia. For these nations, famine, poverty, and underdevelopment were the most urgent issues.

Pollution from factories and cars was seen as a growing menace

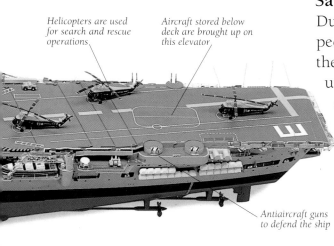

Helicopters are used for search and rescue operations

Aircraft stored below deck are brought up on this elevator

Antiaircraft guns to defend the ship

Saving the planet

During the 1970s many people became aware that the Earth's environment was under threat. The decimation of rain forests by logging companies and air pollution caused by industry and automobiles brought a Green agenda to the world's attention.

Male and female clothing, 1940s

DAILY LIFE 1942–1989

WORLD POPULATION

In 1940 the world's population was 2.295 billion people. Fifty years later it had more than doubled to 5.295 billion, largely as a result of better food supplies and improved health facilities. The life expectancy of people has risen in each decade since 1945 by an average of five years. However, this massive growth in the population is not shared equally across the world. Far more people are being born in the poorer "Third World" countries of Africa and Asia than in the richer countries of Europe and America. Yet 90 out of every 1,000 babies born in Tanzania will die before the age of one, compared with just 7 in Japan. Those who survive in Tanzania expect to live to an average age of 51.4. In Japan they will live to be 75.

THE AFFLUENT SOCIETY

While the Third World has continued to remain in poverty and debt, the First World of America, Europe, Australasia, and eastern Asia has seen a massive rise in its standard of living. Most people now own cars, phones, television sets, and other consumer goods, and take at least one vacation each year. Yet this wealth is not shared evenly throughout each country, and many people remain poor in the midst of great affluence.

Male and female clothing, 1980s

TO THE MOON

The launch of an artificial satellite by Russia in 1957, and the achievement of sending a person into space in 1961, prompted a space race with the US to get the first person onto the Moon. The successful mission of *Apollo 11* in 1969 marked the end of the race, and attention has now turned away from the Moon toward unmanned exploration of the Solar System.

Apollo spacecraft, 1972

Television, 1950s

TELEVISION

The introduction of a regular color television service in the US in 1954 and the availability of cheap color TVs marked the start of the television era. Around the world, radio declined in popularity, while the numbers going to the movies slowly fell back from their peak in the early 1950s. During the 1980s, satellite and cable TV greatly multiplied the number of channels viewers can watch.

NEW MATERIALS

New materials, such as nylon and plastics, transformed peoples' lives during this period. Such everyday items as nylon hose, rubber gloves, and plastic food containers are all products made from synthetic materials unthought of a century ago.

ROCK MUSIC

Ever since 1954, when Bill Haley and the Comets exhorted people to *Rock Around the Clock* and Elvis Presley recorded his first record, rock 'n' roll has been the music of youth. By the 1970s rock music was big business; in the 1980s it focused attention on world issues such as the famine in eastern Africa.

Nylon hose

Jukebox, 1950s

1942

ARTS AND ENTERTAINMENT

•1942 WHITE CHRISTMAS

The otherwise unremarkable film *Holiday Inn* will always be remembered for one song – *White Christmas*, written by Irving Berlin and sung by Bing Crosby. The song reappeared as the title song of a 1954 film starring Crosby, Danny Kaye, and Rosemary Clooney. *White Christmas* went on to become one of the biggest-selling records of all time.

Bing Crosby

•1943 OKLAHOMA!

With music by Richard Rodgers and lyrics by Oscar Hammerstein, the musical *Oklahoma!* opened in New York in March. With songs such as *Oh, What A Beautiful Morning*, the musical was an instant hit, confirming Rodgers and Hammerstein as America's greatest composers of musicals.

•1944 GLEN MILLER

The American bandleader, famous for such songs as *In The Mood* and *Moonlight Serenade*, went missing on a flight from London to Paris in December 1944. His plane was never found. During the war, Miller played regularly for Allied troops.

Glen Miller (left)

SCIENCE AND DISCOVERY

•1942 FIRST REACTOR

The world's first nuclear reactor capable of producing electricity was built at the University of Chicago by the Italian scientist Enrico Fermi. The reactor was known as an atomic pile because it consisted of a pile of carbon blocks and radioactive uranium.

•1942 MANHATTAN PROJECT

President Roosevelt set up the Manhattan Project in August 1942 to build atomic weapons. With a huge budget, scientists from America and Britain worked for three years at Los Alamos in the New Mexico desert under the leadership of Robert Oppenheimer. Using pure uranium and plutonium obtained by research laboratories elsewhere in the US, they constructed three atomic bombs.

Scuba diver

•1943 SCUBA GEAR

In 1943 Frenchmen Jacques Yves Cousteau and Emil Gagnan solved the problem of supplying air to divers by inventing the Self-Contained Underwater Breathing Apparatus (SCUBA). Scuba divers carry cylinders of compressed air strapped to their backs.

•1944 V-2 ROCKET

Toward the end of World War II, German scientist Werner von Braun perfected a 15-ton rocket capable of delivering a one-ton warhead to a target more than 200 miles (320 km) away at a speed of 3,500 mph (5,600 km/h). The V-2 rocket (also known as the A4) was the first long-range guided missile.

A V-2 leaves the launch pad

EVERYDAY LIFE

•1942 HOME FRONT

With all men of fighting age conscripted into the armed services, women across Europe and America were called on to work in factories and on the land, and to run essential services such as transportation and postal deliveries. Because of the fear of gas attacks, everyone in Britain, and all those in France who lived in towns and cities, were issued gas masks.

Civilians clearing bomb damage in a German town

•1944 BOMBING

Early in the war, German bombers inflicted huge damage on European cities. In 1940–41 the Blitz almost destroyed central London. The Allies began bombing raids on German cities in 1942, using as many as 1,000 bombers in a single raid. In 1945, more than 80,000 civilians were killed during the fire-bombing of Dresden.

Fitting gas masks in a British school

WORLD EVENTS

•1942 WORLD WAR II

- January – German leaders discuss the "Final Solution" – the mass extermination of more than 6 million Jews.
- February – Japanese capture Singapore.
- June – US warplanes defeat the Japanese fleet at the Battle of Midway, halting the Japanese offensive in the Pacific.
- July – German troops begin siege of Stalingrad.
- October/November – British Eighth Army under General Montgomery stops the German advance across North Africa toward Egypt at El Alamein in the Libyan desert.
- November – British and US forces land in Morocco and Algeria and begin to advance toward the retreating German army in Libya.

•1943 WORLD WAR II

- January – The German Sixth Army under Field Marshal von Paulus surrenders at Stalingrad after a siege lasting six months. Stalingrad marked the farthest advance of the German army into Russia.
- February – American forces expel the Japanese from the strategically important island of Guadalcanal.
- May – Germans and Italians are expelled from North Africa.
- July – Allied armies invade Sicily; Mussolini resigns as Italian leader.
- July – Massive German tank attack at Kursk on the Russian front is stopped by the Russian army, which then begins to drive the Germans slowly out of Russia.
- September – Allied troops land in southern Italy and begin to advance northward toward Rome.
- November – Allied leaders Roosevelt, Churchill, and Stalin meet in Tehran, Persia, to plan the invasion of western Europe.

USSR Order of the Red Star

Russian troops defend Stalingrad

•1944 WORLD WAR II

- January – Siege of Leningrad broken; during the two-year siege more than 630,000 civilians died of cold and hunger.
- June – Allied troops enter Rome.
- June – Allied troops land on the Normandy beaches of France in the biggest sea invasion ever attempted.

1945

Edith Piaf

•1945 CHARLIE PARKER

The American jazz saxophonist Charlie Parker turned jazz upside down in 1945. Parker developed a new style of jazz, called bop, which allowed musicians to improvise (make up) new melodies in the course of a song instead of merely playing around with the existing melody.

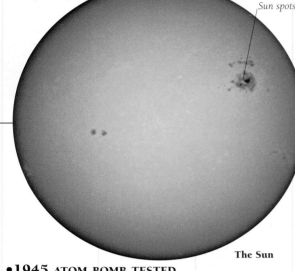

Sun spots

The Sun

•1945 ATOM BOMB TESTED

.On July 16, Manhattan Project scientists detonated the first atomic bomb – a plutonium device code-named "Trinity" – at a test site near Alamogordo in the New Mexico desert. The resulting explosion was equivalent to 22,000 tons (20,000 tonnes) of conventional high-explosive.

•1945 VE/VJ DAY

The ending of the war in Europe in May 1945, and in Asia in August, was the cause of great celebrations. Victory parties were held in every town, and individual families celebrated as soldiers came back from the war. For many people, however, the ending of war meant homelessness and poverty, as many homes and factories had been destroyed.

A VE Day celebration

•1945 WORLD WAR II

• March – Allied troops cross Rhine and head for Berlin.
• April – Roosevelt dies and is succeeded as US president by Harry Truman.
• April – As Russian troops enter suburbs of Berlin, Hitler commits suicide.
• August – US drops atomic bombs on Hiroshima and Nagasaki, leading to Japanese surrender.

•1945 END OF WORLD WAR II

More than 50 million people died worldwide as a result of World War II; for the first time in warfare, more civilians than soldiers lost their lives. Russia suffered the worst, with more than 20 million deaths, while Poland lost 6 million people, 15% of its entire population, including 3 million Jews.

•1946 EDITH PIAF

French songstress Edith Piaf began singing in Parisian bars at the age of only 15, and soon established herself as an international cabaret star. Her most famous song – *La Vie En Rose* – was recorded in 1946, and did much to revive French morale after the end of the war.

•1946 SUN SPOT RADIO WAVES

The discovery that sun spots send out radio waves was made by British scientists Edward Appleton and Donald Hay. This discovery explains why sun-spot activity produces various disturbances, such as aurora, magnetic storms, and interference with radio reception, on Earth.

•1946 FIRST COMPUTER

American scientists constructed an Electronic Numerical Integrator And Calculator (ENIAC), the world's first automatic, general-purpose, electronic computer. ENIAC, which consisted of more than 18,000 valves, filled an entire room and could handle 5,000 calculations per second.

"Mushroom" cloud produced by the atomic bomb at Hiroshima, 1945

•1946 WAR CRIME TRIALS

In April 1946, a series of trials started in Tokyo against 28 Japanese leaders accused of war crimes. Similar trials had begun the previous November in Nuremberg against 21 German leaders. The trials found most of the accused guilty, sentencing both Japanese and German leaders to death or imprisonment.

•1946 UNITED NATIONS

Fifty-one nations signed the 1945 UN charter, which set up a security council and a range of specialized agencies to deal with world problems. The first meeting of the United Nations General Assembly took place in London in January 1946.

•1947 LA PESTE

French author Albert Camus is one of the most important writers of the 20th century. In a series of novels, essays, and plays, including *La Peste* (The Plague, 1947), Camus spelled out the philosophy of existentialism. Existentialists believe that human beings have free will to make their own decisions and create their own destinies.

•1947 METHOD ACTING

In New York, a group of theater directors founded the Actors' Studio to promote method acting. Method actors base their performances on emotional experiences rather than on technical expertise.

•1947 CARBON-14 DATING

Working at the Institute of Nuclear Studies in Chicago, Illinois, Willard Libby discovered that carbon-14 can be used to date organic remains such as plants, trees, and animal bones. Carbon-14 is a radioactive isotope of the element carbon, which is produced by living things.

•1947 NEW LOOK

In reaction to the dull clothing of the war years, the French fashion designer Christian Dior launched a "New Look" at the spring fashion show in Paris.

The "New Look" for women, 1947

Nehru signs the independence document

•1947 INDIA BECOMES INDEPENDENT

India became independent in August 1947 with Jawaharlal Nehru as prime minister. The Muslim states of India became independent in their own right as Pakistan. Ceylon (now Sri Lanka) and Burma received their independence from Britain in 1948.

ARTS AND ENTERTAINMENT

•1948
FIRST LP
By making the grooves on the disk narrower, slowing the turntable speed to 33$\frac{1}{3}$ revolutions-per-minute, and making the disks from unbreakable plastic rather than brittle shellac, CBS Records produced a long-playing record that contained up to 15 minutes of music on each side. Later developments extended that time to 25 minutes, allowing popular musicians the opportunity to compose and record lengthy pieces of music.

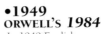

George Orwell

•1949
ORWELL'S *1984*
In 1949 English writer George Orwell's prophetic novel *1984* was published. In it, he described a gloomy future ruled by a dictator called "Big Brother" and his sinister "Thought Police".

•1950
ABSTRACT ART
By 1950 the major movement in modern art was Abstract Expressionism, based in New York. Artists such as Jackson Pollock, Mark Rothko, and Willem de Kooning painted huge canvases that contained few recognizable objects or people. Jackson Pollock achieved notoriety by dripping paint onto a canvas with a stick or straight from the can.

SCIENCE AND DISCOVERY

•1948 TRANSISTOR
Bell Laboratories announced in 1948 that three of its researchers had developed a transistor that could amplify (increase the strength of) a radio signal by more than 100 times. The first transistor was made of a piece of a metallike chemical called germanium and was far more compact than existing radio valves. Today most electronic devices use transistors.

The first transistor, 1949

•1949
SIMONE DE BEAUVOIR
The publication of *The Second Sex* by French writer Simone de Beauvoir was a landmark of feminist thinking. In her book she analyzed the social and cultural conditions that make women second-class citizens. De Beauvoir's ideas have been extremely influential worldwide.

Untitled – a painting by Mark Rothko

•1950
MYXOMATOSIS
In Australia, the viral disease myxomatosis was artificially introduced to keep the rabbit population down. Ironically, rabbits were not themselves native to Australia, having been first introduced as pets.

•1950
DEEP-SEA LIFE
Danish scientists on board *SS Galathea* discovered living organisms some 34,000 ft (10,360 m) below the Pacific Ocean. Until then it had been thought impossible for living creatures to survive the water pressure at such depths.

EVERYDAY LIFE

•1948
MICROWAVE OVEN
The idea for the microwave oven came to an American, Percy LeBaron Spencer, when a chocolate bar melted in his pocket as he stood in front of a magnetron, the electronic tube at the heart of a radar transmitter. He guessed that the microwaves generated by the tube had melted the bar, and became convinced that microwaves could be used for cooking. The first microwave oven was produced in 1948, although microwaves suitable for the home did not make their appearance until 1955.

Microwave oven

•1948 POST-WAR PROBLEMS
Conditions after the war remained difficult for most people. Many goods were in short supply, rationing continued, and there was little money available to repair bomb damage.

•1950 CREDIT CARD
The world's first credit card – a plastic card enabling people to buy goods or services and pay for them later – was invented by American businessman Ralph Schneider. In 1950 he devised the Diners' Club card, which enabled people in New York to eat out in any of 27 restaurants and settle the bill at the end of the month.

United Nations Korean War medal

WORLD EVENTS

•1948
BERLIN AIRLIFT
In an effort to end allied control over half the divided city of Berlin, Russian troops cut off access to the city from western Germany. British and US planes flew in supplies until the blockade was lifted in 1949.

•1948 ISRAEL
The independent Jewish state of Israel came into existence on May 14, 1948, and had to fight for its survival against invading Arab armies.

Mao Zedong

•1949
CHINESE REPUBLIC UNDER MAO
After years of civil war, the Communist Party, led by Mao Zedong, took control of mainland China, forcing the nationalist government of Chiang Kai-shek to retreat to the offshore island of Taiwan.

•1949 DIVISION OF GERMANY
The British, French, and US zones of occupied Germany joined together to form the German Federal Republic, with a capital in Bonn. The Russian zone became the German Democratic Republic, with a capital in East Berlin.

•1949 NATO FORMED
Eleven western nations, including Britain, US, and France, signed the North Atlantic Treaty in April 1949. The treaty set up a defensive military alliance against the threat of a Russian invasion.

•1950–1953 KOREAN WAR
After the defeat of Japan in 1945, Korea was divided into the Russian–sponsored north, and the US–sponsored south. War broke out in 1950 when the northern armies invaded the south. The United Nations sent an international army that forced the northern armies back to the border with China. A ceasefire was signed in July 1953 that permanently divided Korea into two halves.

American soldiers in Korea

1951

•1951 MARLON BRANDO

US film star Marlon Brando shot to fame in a film adaptation of the Tennessee Williams play *A Streetcar Named Desire*. Brando's smoldering portrayal of Stanley Kowalski made him a huge international star. His later films include *The Godfather* (1972) and *Apocalypse Now* (1979).

Marlon Brando, 1951

•1952 JOHN CAGE

Musician John Cage pushed modern music to its limits in *4'33"*, which consisted of silence. Cage believed that the point of a musical performance was the activity of the performers and the attention of the listeners, rather than any music that might be performed.

•1952 "ROCK 'N' ROLL"

American disk-jockey Alan Freed coined a new term when he began to play black American music to his predominately white audience on a radio program entitled *Moondog's Rock 'n' Roll Party*. Rock 'n' roll quickly became the label attached to rhythm-and-blues music.

•1953 LE CORBUSIER

Swiss architect Le Corbusier revolutionized town planning by proposing new cities where people would live in apartment towers surrounded by open spaces. Le Corbusier put his ideas into practice in Marseilles, France, where in 1953 he built *Unité d'Habitation*, a vertical city for 1,600 people.

Unité d'Habitation, Marseilles

•1952 H-BOMBS

The thermonuclear hydrogen bomb (H-bomb) is much more powerful than an atomic bomb. The first H-bomb was exploded by American scientists on the mid-Pacific atoll of Eniwetok in November 1952.

•1953 DNA

Molecules of deoxyribonucleic acid (DNA) are found in all plants and animals. In 1953 the British scientists Francis Crick and James Watson identified the structure of DNA as consisting of millions of atoms arranged in a twisted double spiral (or double helix), and discovered that DNA molecules carry the blueprint for life. The pair won the 1962 Nobel Prize for medicine for their work.

•1951 PEACEFUL USE OF ATOMIC ENERGY

Electricity was experimentally produced from an atomic reactor in Akron, Idaho, in December 1951. Three years later, an atomic reactor in the Russian city of Obninsk generated 5 megawatts of electricity, enough for about 5,000 people. Today, more than 400 nuclear power plants produce about one-sixth of the world's power, although there are serious doubts about their effects on the environment.

Comet jet airliner

Structure of DNA

•1952 FIRST JET AIRLINER

The world's first jet airliner was the 48-passenger De Havilland Comet 1, which had four turbojet engines mounted in its wings. The Comet's structural weaknesses led to a series of crashes; however, the improved Comet 4 became the first jet to enter regular transatlantic service.

•1952 TRANSISTOR RADIO

With the development of the transistor, it was possible to produce a miniaturized, portable radio powered by batteries. An early prototype of a transistor radio was produced in 1952, although it did not go on general sale for another two years. Unlike valve radios, which took several minutes to warm up, transistor radios came to life immediately.

Transistor radio

Twin strands of DNA are linked by chemicals called base pairs

•1953 OPEN-HEART SURGERY

In the US, surgeon J. Gibbon performed the first open-heart operation, paving the way for huge advances in preventing heart disease. By 1967 surgeons were able to transplant human hearts from one person to another.

•1951 US-JAPAN PEACE TREATY

A peace treaty was signed in San Francisco between Japan and 49 nations in September 1951. The treaty, which came into force in April 1952, ended the military occupation by Allied troops led by US general Douglas MacArthur. It led to a period of close cooperation between Japan and the US.

•1951 CHURCHILL ELECTED

Winston Churchill first became British prime minister at the height of war in 1940, when he was chosen to lead an all-party government. He then lost power in 1945, when a Labour government was elected by a massive majority. Churchill returned to 10 Downing Street in 1951, at the age of 77, when he led the Conservative Party to victory in the general election.

•1951 LIBYA INDEPENDENT

Previously an Italian colony, Libya was occupied by British troops in 1942, and remained under British control for nine years. In September 1951 Libya became the first African state to receive its independence from European rule in the post-war period.

Tensing and Hillary

•1952 EVA PERÓN DIES

Eva Perón, the wife of the Argentinean leader Juan Perón, was idolized by the population for her common sense and her support for poor people. Her death in 1952 was mourned by the whole nation.

•1953 EVEREST CONQUERED

On June 1, 1953, the New Zealand climber Edmund Hillary and Tensing Norgay (far left), a Nepalese Sherpa tribesman guide, became the first people to climb Mt. Everest, the highest mountain in the world at 29,028 ft (8,848 m).

•1953 STALIN DIES

After almost 30 years as the leader of Soviet Russia, Josef Stalin died at the age of 73 on March 5, 1953. His death was followed by a bitter internal power-struggle between rival politicians, and he was eventually succeeded by Nikita Khruschev. Three years later, Khruschev publically attacked Stalin's record, and condemned the cult of personality surrounding him.

1954

ARTS AND ENTERTAINMENT

•1954
ELVIS PRESLEY

In July 1954, a 19-year-old boy recorded his first record. The song, *That's All Right*, was a moderate success, but its singer, Elvis Aron Presley, soon attracted attention for his energetic performances. His first big hit, *Heartbreak Hotel* in 1956, turned him into an international symbol of rock music. Presley sold more than 300 million records worldwide before his death in 1977.

Elvis Presley

•1955
DISNEYLAND OPENS

On July 18, 1955, the film-maker Walt Disney opened a theme park based on his cartoon films at Anaheim, California. The 150-acre site, which cost more than $17 million to build, included a reconstruction of Sleeping Beauty's castle. In 1971 Disney World opened in Orlando, Florida.

Whaam! by Roy Lichtenstein

•1956 POP ART

An exhibition at the Whitechapel Art Gallery, London, entitled *This Is Tomorrow*, introduced the world to Pop Art. The new art, which quickly spread to the US, used objects such as soup cans and comic strips in paintings to challenge the seriousness of most modern art. Famous Pop artists included Roy Lichtenstein and Andy Warhol.

SCIENCE AND DISCOVERY

•1954
"FLYING BEDSTEAD"

The world's first vertical takeoff and landing (VTOL) aircraft took to the skies in 1954. The prototype was nicknamed the "Flying Bedstead" because of its ungainly appearance. Its success proved that it was possible to design an engine able to direct its thrust both downward, to push the aircraft vertically off the ground, and forward, to propel it through the air in the usual manner.

"Flying Bedstead"

•1955 START OF THE SPACE RACE

In 1955 the United Nations announced that 1957–58 would be designated International Geophysical Year (IGY). Both the US and the USSR announced their intention to launch satellites into space during the IGY, thus beginning a space race between the two nations.

Battery   *Timing circuits*

Heart pacemaker

•1956 PACEMAKER

With the development of the transistor in the 1950s, it became possible to produce the pacemaker – an electrical device to stimulate and control the beat of the human heart. Pacemakers are small enough to be implanted under a patient's skin.

EVERYDAY LIFE

•1954 FIRST SHOPPING MALL

The idea of locating a range of shops, banks, and other services and entertainments in an enclosed shopping mall on the outskirts of town was first realized in Northland, north of Detroit, Michigan. By the mid-1980s, shopping malls accounted for more than 50% of all US retail sales. Today it is increasingly recognized that shopping malls and other out-of-town shopping centers can damage the social life of a town.

Rosa Parkes (front)

•1955 ROSA PARKES

Some southern states of the US were segregated – black Americans were forbidden to sit with white people in restaurants and other public places. Rosa Parkes, a black woman from Montgomery, Alabama, refused to sit in the black-only seats of a local bus. A boycott of city buses, which had widespread support, achieved desegregation the following year.

1956 Hungarians revolt

WORLD EVENTS

French troops in Vietnam

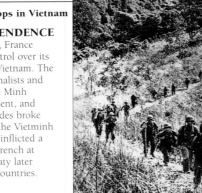

•1954
VIETNAMESE INDEPENDENCE

At the end of World War II, France struggled to reestablish control over its Southeast Asian colony of Vietnam. The Vietminh coalition of nationalists and Communists led by Ho Chi Minh declared Vietnam independent, and fighting between the two sides broke out in 1946. In May 1954 the Vietminh army, led by General Giap, inflicted a humiliating defeat on the French at Dien Bien Phu. A peace treaty later divided Vietnam into two countries.

•1954
NASSER IN POWER

After the fall of the Egyptian monarchy in 1952 and the declaration of a republic, a number of people jostled for power. In November 1954 Colonel Gamal Abdel Nasser took control and was elected president of Egypt. Nasser ruled Egypt until 1970, leading Egypt and the wider Arab world against both Israel and western influence in Arab affairs.

•1955
WARSAW PACT

In response to the establishment of the US-dominated NATO defense organization in 1949, the USSR formed an alliance of European Communist states known as the Warsaw Pact. Under the terms of the pact, Russian troops and tanks were stationed throughout Eastern Europe.

•1955 NON-ALIGNED NATIONS

At the instigation of President Sukarno of Indonesia, representatives of 29 Asian and African nations met in Bandung, Indonesia, to adopt a neutral, non-aligned attitude to the Cold War between the US and USSR, and to champion anti-colonialism in the two continents. The Bandung Conference marked the start of an international movement for the Third World.

•1956 HUNGARY INVADED

Hungary had been occupied by Soviet troops since 1945, and had become a Communist state in 1949. In 1956, Hungary attempted to leave the Warsaw Pact and become a neutral state free of Russian control. Russian troops invaded the country in November, crushing the rebellion and executing its leaders.

•1956 SUEZ CRISIS

Egypt's leader, Nasser, nationalized the Suez Canal, which was owned by the British government and French investors. In collusion with the Israelis, British and French forces invaded Egypt. After an international outcry, Britain and France withdrew, and Egypt kept control of the canal.

1957

•1957 ON THE ROAD

In his novel *On The Road*, American author Jack Kerouac summed up the mood of the Beat Generation – young people disillusioned by life in the US in the 1950s. The book describes a journey across America by a group of rootless young people who have dropped out of the rat-race of daily life.

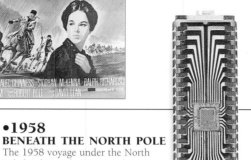

Dr. Zhivago film poster

•1958 DR. ZHIVAGO

The publication of *Dr. Zhivago* brought international acclaim to its Russian author, Boris Pasternak. The novel describes a love affair at the time of the Russian Revolution.

•1959 FOUNDATION OF MOTOWN RECORDS

Detroit songwriter Berry Gordy set up Tamla Motown Records in 1959 to record local black rhythm-and-blues singers. Within a few years he had established a number of singers, including the Supremes, the Four Tops, Marvin Gaye, and Stevie Wonder, who dominated American and international popular music during the 1960s.

SRN-1 hovercraft

•1957 SPUTNIK 1

On October 4, the USSR beat the US in the space race by launching an artificial satellite into space. *Sputnik 1* weighed 184 lb (83.4 kg) and circled the Earth every 95 minutes. The US launched its first satellite, *Explorer I*, three months later.

•1957 ENDOSCOPE

Three US scientists developed the flexible fiber-optic endoscope to enable doctors to look inside a human body without having to perform an operation. The endoscope consists of a length of optical fibers through which light can travel. Once the endoscope is inserted inside the body, the doctor looks through the eyepiece to make a diagnosis.

•1958 BENEATH THE NORTH POLE

The 1958 voyage under the North Pole by the nuclear-powered submarine *USS Nautilus* proved that there was no land underneath the Arctic ice cap. Beneath the South Pole, however, there is the continent of Antarctica.

Microchip

•1959 HOVERCRAFT

The idea that a craft could ride on a cushion of air over both land and sea had been demonstrated by the British inventor Christopher Cockerell in 1955. In 1959 the world's first full-sized hovercraft, the Cockerell-designed SRN–1, traveled across the English Channel.

•1959 MICROCHIP

Bob Noyce of Fairchild Semiconductor, US, printed an entire electronic circuit on top of a single crystal, or "microchip," of silicon using a photographic process. This breakthrough enabled the computer revolution to begin.

•1957 GOOD TIMES

For many people during the 1950s, the post-war prosperity enjoyed by America and western Europe led to a big increase in their standard of living. Wages rose, prices remained low, and labor-saving devices, such as washing machines and vacuum cleaners, could be afforded by most people.

•1959 MINI CAR

Designed by Alec Issigonis, the Mini was a masterpiece of industrial design. With its extraordinary compactness, economy, and performance, the Mini set a precedent followed by all small cars today. More than one million Minis had been sold by the end of 1965.

Mini Cooper car

This car has been modified for motor racing

Kwame Nkrumah

•1957 GHANA

The British colony of the Gold Coast became the first black African nation to receive its independence from European rule. The independence of Ghana in 1957 under the leadership of Kwame Nkrumah began a process that was to lead to self-government for all of Africa by 1990.

•1957 MALAYA

Britain began to withdraw from Southeast Asia in 1957 when it granted independence to Malaya. Six years later, two British colonies in Borneo were added to Malaya to create the state of Malaysia. The city of Singapore became independent in 1965.

Charles de Gaulle

•1958 ALGERIAN REVOLT

Led by the National Liberation Front (FLN), Algerian nationalists had begun to fight for independence in 1954. The French army responded with enormous brutality, causing the deaths of more than 1 million Algerians. In 1958, believing that Algeria was to be granted independence, the European settlers overthrew the French government.

•1958 DE GAULLE

The collapse of the French government in May 1958 led to a major crisis in France. The crisis was solved by the recall from retirement of the French liberation leader Charles de Gaulle to head a new government of "national safety."

•1959 FIDEL CASTRO

After three years of open rebellion, Cuban nationalists led by Fidel Castro overthrew the corrupt government of President Fulgencio Batistá and took control of the island. Castro was initially supported by the US, but he turned to China and the USSR for support in 1960. As a result, the US waged a campaign of economic sanctions against Cuba, and attempted to overthrow Castro by force.

Fidel Castro

1960

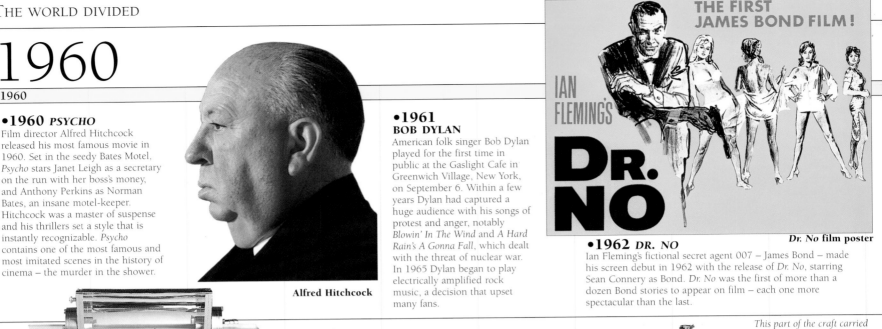

THE FIRST JAMES BOND FILM!

IAN FLEMING'S

DR. NO

Dr. No film poster

ARTS AND ENTERTAINMENT

•1960 PSYCHO

Film director Alfred Hitchcock released his most famous movie in 1960. Set in the seedy Bates Motel, *Psycho* stars Janet Leigh as a secretary on the run with her boss's money, and Anthony Perkins as Norman Bates, an insane motel-keeper. Hitchcock was a master of suspense and his thrillers set a style that is instantly recognizable. *Psycho* contains one of the most famous and most imitated scenes in the history of cinema – the murder in the shower.

Alfred Hitchcock

•1961 BOB DYLAN

American folk singer Bob Dylan played for the first time in public at the Gaslight Cafe in Greenwich Village, New York, on September 6. Within a few years Dylan had captured a huge audience with his songs of protest and anger, notably *Blowin' In The Wind* and *A Hard Rain's A Gonna Fall*, which dealt with the threat of nuclear war. In 1965 Dylan began to play electrically amplified rock music, a decision that upset many fans.

•1962 DR. NO

Ian Fleming's fictional secret agent 007 – James Bond – made his screen debut in 1962 with the release of *Dr. No*, starring Sean Connery as Bond. *Dr. No* was the first of more than a dozen Bond stories to appear on film – each one more spectacular than the last.

SCIENCE AND DISCOVERY

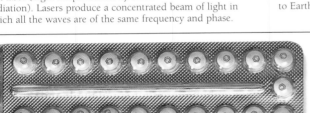

Ruby laser, mid-1960s

Ruby crystal

•1960 LASER

By passing a beam of light through a rod of synthetic ruby, US scientist Theodore Maiman constructed the world's first laser (Light Amplification by Stimulated Emission of Radiation). Lasers produce a concentrated beam of light in which all the waves are of the same frequency and phase.

•1961 FIRST MAN IN SPACE

On April 12, a 27-year-old Russian air force pilot, Yuri Alexeyevitch Gagarin, became the first person in space when he orbited the Earth in a *Vostok* spacecraft. The craft, which weighed 4.5 tons (4 tonnes), was launched from a site in central Asia. Gagarin reached a height of 190 miles (305 km) during his single orbit before returning gently to Earth by parachute.

Vostok spacecraft

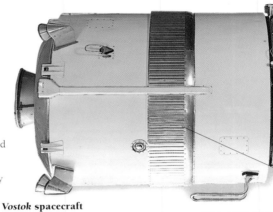

This part of the craft carried Gagarin back to Earth

This part of the craft contained engines and life-support systems

EVERYDAY LIFE

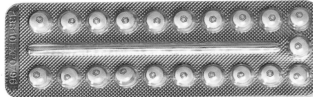

Pack of contraceptive pills

•1960 WEATHER FORECASTING

The daily weather forecast improved in accuracy throughout the 1960s after the launch of *Tiros 1*, the world's first specialized weather satellite.

•1961 THE PILL

The world's first contraceptive pill went on general sale in the US following several years of medical trials. The pill works by inhibiting the release of hormones required for ovulation in the same way hormones produced naturally during pregnancy prevent further conception. The pill allowed women to control their own fertility and gave them more control over their bodies.

•1962 TELSTAR

Transcontinental television became a reality with the launch of the *Telstar* satellite from Cape Canaveral, in Florida. The satellite circled the Earth every 157.8 minutes, allowing live television pictures to be transmitted across the Atlantic between America and Europe.

Solar panel from *Telstar*

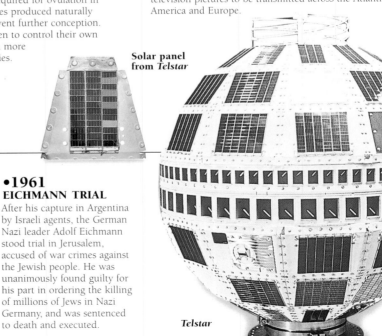

Telstar

WORLD EVENTS

•1960 THE CONGO

A Belgian colony since 1908, the Belgian Congo became independent in 1960. However the country was ill-prepared to govern itself, and quickly fell apart as the copper-rich province of Katanga declared itself independent. The United Nations sent troops to restore order, and Colonel Mobutu took over as leader after a military coup in 1965. In 1971 Mobutu renamed the country Zaire.

•1960 U-2 INCIDENT

After the death of Stalin in 1953, relations between the USSR and the US slowly began to improve. However, a summit conference held in 1960 between the Russian, US, French, and British leaders was wrecked by the shooting down of an American U-2 spy plane over Russia. US president Eisenhower refused to apologize for spying, and the incident led to increased rivalry between the two superpowers.

The wall divided families and friends

•1961 EICHMANN TRIAL

After his capture in Argentina by Israeli agents, the German Nazi leader Adolf Eichmann stood trial in Jerusalem, accused of war crimes against the Jewish people. He was unanimously found guilty for his part in ordering the killing of millions of Jews in Nazi Germany, and was sentenced to death and executed.

•1961 BERLIN WALL

As the economic differences widened between East and West Germany, more and more people left the east to seek a better standard of life in the west. In August 1961 the East German authorities erected a wall along the divided city of Berlin, closing the last gap in the frontier between the two states. The Berlin Wall symbolized the division of Europe into two rival camps.

•1962 CUBAN MISSILE CRISIS

The world came to the brink of nuclear war in October 1962 when the USSR began to install missiles with atomic warheads on Cuba. After intense negotiations, the USSR agreed to withdraw its missiles if the US lifted its blockade of Cuba and promised not to invade the island.

1963

1963

•1963 THE FIRE NEXT TIME

Many of the novels of African-American writer James Baldwin deal with the racial tension he experienced during his early years in New York. An active member of the civil rights movement, he wrote the essay *The Fire Next Time* in 1963 as a warning to white America: solve the problem of racial division or face the violent consequences.

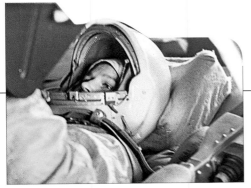

Valentina Tereshkova

•1963 FIRST WOMAN IN SPACE

After the US sent an astronaut into space in February 1962, the space race between the US and the USSR intensified as each country aimed to land a person on the Moon. Meanwhile, the USSR achieved another first when Lieutenant Valentina Tereshkova became the first woman in space in June 1963.

•1963 CASSETTE RECORDER

The development of the cassette tape recorder by the Dutch company Phillips created a revolution in the music industry. Phillips patented the idea in 1963, but then cleverly allowed other companies to copy it, ensuring the tape became the world standard. Cassette tapes allowed people to both listen to and record music, playing back the results on compact, portable machines.

John F. Kennedy

•1963 KENNEDY SHOT

John F. Kennedy became the 35th and youngest president of the United States in 1960. His youth and vigor made him a symbol of hope and inspiration across the world. These hopes were shattered upon his assassination by Lee Harvey Oswald in Dallas, Texas, on November 22, 1963. To this day, whether Oswald was acting alone or as part of a wider conspiracy has never been proved.

The Beatles, 1964

•1964 BEATLEMANIA

John, Paul, George, and Ringo were already famous in Britain for topping the music charts in 1963. But it was not until *I Want To Hold Your Hand* entered the US charts in early 1964 that the Beatles became international pop stars.

•1964 UNDERSTANDING MEDIA

The Canadian academic Marshall McLuhan predicted that satellite communications would shrink the world into one large global village where everyone would have access to the same information. Television would be so dominant that it was not the message it contained that was important, but the medium of television itself. His most important work expressing these views was *Understanding Media* (1964).

"Bullet train"

•1964 "BULLET TRAIN"

The world-famous Japanese "bullet train" first went into service on the electric Shinkansen high-speed railroad between Tokyo and Osaka in 1964. The 12-car trains traveled at speeds of up to 130 mph (210 km/h). Passengers enjoyed a smooth ride, good sound insulation, and comfortable, open-plan cars with aircraft-style seats.

Viet Cong soldier

•1964 PLO FORMED

In order to bring the various exiled Palestinian groups together, the Palestinian Liberation Organization (PLO) was founded in Jordan in May 1964. The PLO soon took responsibility for all Palestinians living in exile and under Israeli rule in the occupied territories.

•1964 CIVIL RIGHTS IN US

Dr. Martin Luther King, Jr. first came to prominence as the leader of the 1955 bus boycott in Montgomery, Alabama. By the mid-1960s, he was the leader of a national campaign to achieve civil rights for black people. After more than 250,000 people led by Dr. King marched on Washington in August 1963 to demand an end to racial discrimination, the US government introduced a Civil Rights Bill. In July 1964, the bill was signed into law by President Lyndon B. Johnson.

•1965 THE SOUND OF MUSIC

Julie Andrews and Christopher Plummer turned Rodgers and Hammerstein's Broadway musical *The Sound of Music* into one of the most popular and successful films of all time.

•1965 ROLLING STONES

The British group the Rolling Stones had their first US number one hit with *Satisfaction* in 1965. Unlike the Beatles, who played pop songs and appealed to the whole family, the Stones played hard-edged rhythm and blues and appealed to more rebellious listeners.

•1965 PICTURES FROM MARS

After a seven-month voyage through space, the US space probe *Mariner 4* sent back the first close-up images of another planet. Although the images were obtained from orbit at a distance of about 6,200 miles (10,000 km), they were detailed enough to show that Mars has a cratered surface like the Moon.

Mini dress

•1965 FASHION

The "Swinging Sixties" brought with them many new fashions, liberating young people from the conservative styles of their parents. Denim jeans and T-shirts became universally popular, while more daring young women wore mini-skirts, often with knee-height boots. Influenced by pop groups such as the Beatles and Rolling Stones, many young men grew their hair long.

•1965–73 VIETNAM WAR

By 1965 South Vietnam was losing its fight against the Communist forces from North Vietnam. The US had been supplying only weapons and military aid, but in 1965, US ground troops were dispatched to Vietnam. By the end of 1966, almost 400,000 US troops were fighting there. The bitter war came to a close in 1975 when the Communists took over South Vietnam.

1966

1966   1967

ARTS AND ENTERTAINMENT

•1966 *THE MAGUS*

John Fowles's novel about magic on the Greek island of Phraxos has captivated readers ever since it was published in 1966. Its main character, Conchis, hides behind a series of masks, playing games with the people he meets. One of Fowles's later novels, *The French Lieutenant's Woman* (1969), was made into a film starring Meryl Streep.

Gabriel Garciá Márquez

•1967 PSYCHEDELIA

Psychedelic (mind-altering) drugs such as LSD had a huge impact in the 1960s. Psychedelic images – bizarre and brightly colored – adorned everything from T-shirts to record sleeves. Two albums that sum up the psychedelic period are the Beatles' *Sergeant Pepper's Lonely Hearts Club Band* and the Rolling Stones' *Their Satanic Majesties Request*.

•1967 *ONE HUNDRED YEARS OF SOLITUDE*

The Colombian novelist Gabriel Garciá Márquez established his reputation with stories written in a style known as "magic-realism." His most famous book is *One Hundred Years Of Solitude* (1967). Márquez won the Nobel Prize for literature in 1982.

Psychedelic record cover

SCIENCE AND DISCOVERY

•1966 LINK-UP IN SPACE

US astronauts Neil Armstrong and David Scott, on board their US *Gemini 8* spacecraft, linked up successfully with the final stage of their *Agena* rocket launcher on March 17. This was the first successful rendezvous and docking by two craft in space. Docking is a maneuver that has since become a regular part of space missions.

•1967 GREENHOUSE EFFECT

Scientists S. Manabe and R.T. Wetherald were concerned about the increase in carbon dioxide in the atmosphere, caused by pollution from factories and cars. In 1967, they warned of a "greenhouse effect" that might lead to global warming. Today, some scientists believe that the world could be as much as 7°F (4°C) warmer by the year 2050.

Industrial pollution

•1968 PULSAR

British astronomers Jocelyn Bell Burnell and Anthony Hewish first recorded strange signals from a star in 1967. The following year they identified the source as a pulsar, a rapidly spinning neutron star that emits brief, sharp pulses of energy instead of a steady radiation. More than 500 pulsars have since been discovered.

EVERYDAY LIFE

•1966 CONSUMERISM

As a result of campaigning by the consumer advocate Ralph Nader, the US government introduced strict measures to improve the safety of cars. Nader's success marked the start of a continuing campaign to establish and protect the interests of ordinary consumers against the power of big business.

•1967 HIPPIES

Rejecting the conventional values of their parents, hippies celebrated the 1967 "Summer of Love" in extravagant style. They wore flowers in their hair and colorful clothes from around the world, including Moroccan kaftans and Native American beadwork. Hippies preached a gospel of peace, love, and understanding. Drugs played an important part in the movement, as did rock music, which by 1967 was internationally popular.

Hippy and child

•1968 STUDENT UNREST

Discontent with authority led many students to demonstrate on the streets and occupy their colleges in protest at a variety of issues. In France, students led demonstrations that almost overthrew the government in May 1968. In the US, many students campaigned against American involvement in the Vietnam War.

French students, 1968

WORLD EVENTS

•1966 CULTURAL REVOLUTION

Chinese leader Mao Zedong urged his followers to return to basic Communism and to reject liberal and westernizing influences. Groups of young Red Guards were sent out to destroy all traces of western culture. This so-called Cultural Revolution did great damage to China and was stopped in 1968.

•1966 INDIRA GANDHI

Following the death of prime minister Shastri, India's ruling Congress Party elected Indira Gandhi to lead the country. India's first woman prime minister was the daughter of Jawaharlal Nehru, who led the country from independence in 1947 until his death in 1964. Mrs. Gandhi proved a strong leader who did much to modernize India. She remained prime minister, with a short break, until her assassination by extremists in 1984.

•1967 ARAB-ISRAELI WAR

In order to remove the threat of attack or invasion, Israel launched a rapid campaign against neighboring Arab countries. Within six days, the Israeli armed services had destroyed the Arab air forces, invaded the Sinai Peninsula, and captured both the west bank of the Jordan River and the Golan Heights in Syria.

•1968 ASSASSINATION OF DR. KING

The black American civil rights leader Martin Luther King was assassinated on April 4, 1968, while on a visit to Memphis, Tennessee. Dr. King's message of nonviolent protest against racial discrimination had brought hope to millions of poor black Americans denied a vote. His death sparked riots in cities throughout the US.

1969

1969 | 1971

Jimi Hendrix

•1969 WOODSTOCK
More than 300,000 people congregated on a farm at Woodstock, New York, for three days in August 1969 to join in a huge music festival. Among the musicians who performed were The Who, Joe Cocker, and Jimi Hendrix. Despite heavy rain and poor organization, Woodstock was a great success and rapidly became a symbol of 1960s' youth culture.

•1969 SAMUEL BECKETT
Irish playwright and novelist Samuel Beckett combined a sense of the absurd with an overwhelming feeling of anguish and loss in all his works. This combination was most evident in *Waiting For Godot* (1952), one of the most celebrated plays of this century. Beckett was awarded the Nobel Prize for literature in 1969.

•1971 DAVID HOCKNEY
British-born artist David Hockney moved to Los Angeles in the 1960s. There he painted a series of paintings celebrating the beautiful climate and the luxurious lifestyle, including *Portrait of an Artist* (1971), depicting a swimming pool.

•1971 CANNES FILM FESTIVAL
Founded in 1946, the Cannes Film Festival had become the major event in the international film year by 1971. To celebrate its 25th anniversary, it awarded an additional prize. The traditional Grand Prize went to Joseph Losey's *The Go-Between*, and a special prize went to Italian director Luchino Visconti's *Death in Venice*, based on a short story by Thomas Mann and starring Dirk Bogarde.

•1969 FIRST MOON WALK
History was made on July 21, 1969, when the American astronaut Neil Armstrong became the first person to set foot on the Moon. With the words, "That's one small step for a man, one giant leap for mankind," he explored the Moon's surface accompanied by his fellow *Apollo 11* astronaut Edwin "Buzz" Aldrin. Once their mission was accomplished, they rejoined the third astronaut, Michael Collins, who was orbiting the Moon on board *Apollo 11*, and returned to splash down in the Pacific Ocean on July 24.

Chocolate pudding

Cherry drink

Astronauts' "space food"

Tomato soup

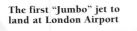

•1970 MOON ROBOT
Although the USSR lost the race with the US to land a person on the Moon, the Soviet space program achieved some notable successes in 1970. The *Luna 17* mission landed the *Lunokhod* robot, which spent several months on the surface sending information back to Earth.

Neil Armstrong on the Moon, 1969

•1971 SPACE STATION
The USSR launched the world's first space station on April 19. Three Russian cosmonauts visited *Salyut 1* for 22 days in June to carry out research in space, although tragically they died during their descent to Earth.

•1971 SUPERTANKER
The world's then largest supertanker, the 410,000-ton (372,000-tonne) *Misseki Maru*, was launched in 1971. The Japanese ship was commissioned to bring oil from the Middle East back to Japan.

•1969 JUMBO JET
Commercial air travel changed dramatically in 1969 with the first flight of the Boeing 747 wide-bodied "Jumbo" jet. The 747 is the world's largest and heaviest aircraft, so large that there is room for an upper and lower deck inside the fuselage. The Jumbo entered regular service across the Atlantic Ocean in 1970, carrying 362 passengers – twice as many as an ordinary jet airliner. Later versions carried even more people.

•1971 POCKET CALCULATOR
Math was made easy with the development of the pocket calculator. By 1971 electronic circuits had become small enough to make calculators that could fit in a pocket, yet still perform complicated calculations at the touch of a few buttons.

One of the first pocket calculators, 1971

The first "Jumbo" jet to land at London Airport

•1969 ULSTER TROUBLES
After years of simmering protest against discrimination, violence erupted between the Catholic and Protestant populations of Northern Ireland. British troops were sent to keep the peace. Within a few years the Irish Republican Army (IRA) began a campaign of terrorism against Britain.

•1969 WILLY BRANDT
Willy Brandt became the first Social Democrat chancellor of West Germany in October 1969. He pursued a policy of friendship with East Germany, Poland, and the USSR for which he won the Nobel Peace Prize in 1971.

•1970 CAMBODIA
A pro-American military leader took control of the Southeast Asian nation of Cambodia in 1970. Communist Khmer Rouge guerrillas led by Pol Pot rapidly overran the country and seized the capital, Phnom Penh, in 1975. Under Pol Pot, all intellectuals were killed, and the population of the capital was forced to work in the countryside. The Khmer Rouge were overthrown in 1979 by an invading Vietnamese army. Nearly half the population of 7 million had died in the fighting, famine, and political killings of the previous four years.

•1971 GREENPEACE
Three environmental campaigners – two Americans and one Canadian – formed a committee in 1971 to campaign against the proposed underground testing of nuclear bombs on the remote Alaskan island of Amchitka. The original name of the committee – Don't Make A Wave – was later changed to Greenpeace. It is now the major environmental campaigning organization in the world.

1972

ARTS AND ENTERTAINMENT

•1972 MUNICH OLYMPICS

The 20th Olympic Games, held in Munich, Germany, ended in tragedy when Palestinian terrorists seized 10 Israeli athletes. One escaped, but the other nine were killed in a bungled rescue attempt by the German authorities. In the games themselves, US athlete Mark Spitz won seven gold medals in swimming events.

•1972 CABARET

Liza Minnelli, daughter of singer Judy Garland, became a star in her own right with her portrayal of Sally Bowles in the film *Cabaret*, based on the stage musical by Bob Fosse.

The "rumble in the jungle" – Ali v. Foreman, Zaire, 1974

•1974 MUHAMMAD ALI

American boxer Cassius Clay became world heavyweight champion in 1964. Soon afterward, he converted to Islam and took a new name. Stripped of his title in 1967 for refusing to fight in Vietnam, he regained the crown in 1974 when he defeated George Foreman in Kinshasa, capital of Zaire. Ali retired from boxing in 1981.

Terra-cotta army

SCIENCE AND DISCOVERY

•1972 PIONEER 10

The US space probe *Pioneer 10* was launched on March 2, 1972, from Cape Kennedy and flew past Jupiter in December 1973. By June 1983 it had reached the limits of the Solar System, and continued its flight into outer space. *Pioneer 10* carries a plaque showing the layout of the Sun and planets, the position of the Earth, and a sketch of a man and a woman.

Dish antenna sends information back to Earth

Pioneer 10

Radioactive power source produces electricity

•1973 SMALL IS BEAUTIFUL

In his book *Small Is Beautiful: A Study Of Economics As If People Mattered*, the German economist Ernst Schumacher turned traditional big business ideas on their head. He argued that nations should stop seeking economic growth through a few energy-intensive industries which harmed the environment, and concentrate instead on small local businesses.

Platform shoes, early 1970s

•1974 TOMB DISCOVERED

A group of Chinese farmers digging a well made one of the archaeological finds of the century. They unearthed the mausoleum of Qin, first emperor of China, who ruled in the third century BC. Guarding the tomb was a terra-cotta army more than 6,000 strong, lined up in formation with horses and chariots. Each soldier was individually modeled – a lifelike representation of the first Chinese imperial army.

EVERYDAY LIFE

•1972 CAT SCANS

In order to look inside the skull, British researcher Godfrey Hounsfield developed a computerized axiom tomography (CAT) scanner to provide cross-sectional X-rays of the brain. The scanner takes thousands of X-rays, and then analyzes them so that doctors can see the brain from a variety of angles.

•1973 FASHION

After the 1960s, fashion became even more unisex. Both men and women wore flared pants, embroidered clothes, and platform shoes. For women, hot pants (very short shorts) became popular for a while. For both sexes, and almost all ages, denim jeans and colored T-shirts were almost a uniform. But for those with more adventurous tastes, makeup and streaked hair became fashionable as "glam rock" enjoyed a brief period of popularity.

Bar code

•1974 BAR CODE

Computer-readable product codes, or bar codes, were developed for the US grocery industry during the 1960s. By the mid-1970s, almost every product on sale featured a bar code, enabling shops to monitor their stocks by optically scanning the code as each item was sold. By calculating quantities and types of product sold, shops could reorder products to suit consumer demand.

WORLD EVENTS

Arab–Israeli War, 1974

•1972 SUPERPOWER DETENTE

US president Richard Nixon visited both China and the USSR in 1972 in an attempt to bring the world's three superpowers closer together, a process known as détente. He was the first US president to visit these two countries, ending a generation of hostility between the US and its Communist rivals.

•1973 YOM KIPPUR WAR

Egyptian and Syrian forces launched a surprise attack against Israel, which was caught unprepared celebrating the religious Yom Kippur holiday. The war led to a rapid increase in the price of Middle Eastern oil, prompting price inflation around the world.

•1973 ALLENDE ELECTED

In September 1970 the left-wing politician Salvador Allende was elected president of Chile. There was fierce opposition to his government from big business, supported by the US Central Intelligence Agency. Allende was overthrown by a military coup led by General Pinochet in 1973. Democratic rule was eventually restored to Chile in 1989.

Richard Nixon

•1974 WATERGATE

In the 1972 presidential election, employees of US president Richard Nixon's Republican Party broke into the headquarters of the rival Democratic Party in the Watergate Building in Washington. By 1974 it was clear that Nixon had authorized the break-in, and he was forced to resign in disgrace on August 9. He was the first US president to resign from office.

•1974 DEMOCRACY RETURNS TO PORTUGAL

After almost 50 years of dictatorship, a peaceful military coup on April 25 – which became known as the Revolution of Flowers – led Portugal back to democratic government. Mozambique, Angola, and other Portuguese colonies were soon given their independence.

1975

1975

Jaws, film poster

•1975 JAWS
This story of a shark attacking swimmers at a vacation resort terrified movie audiences around the world. *Jaws* was the work of Steven Spielberg, who has become one of the most successful film directors of all time.

•1975 VIDEO RECORDERS
Video recorders enable viewers to record television programs or play back pre-recorded tapes of films or other images. The first videos were developed in 1956 and were the size of a piano. By 1975, small recorders able to fit beneath a television set were on sale.

Pompidou Centre

•1976 ABBA
The Swedish pop group Abba won the 1974 Eurovision Song Contest with *Waterloo*. By 1976, they had become the best-selling group in Europe, as well as Sweden's biggest export earner after Volvo cars.

•1977 NEW GALLERY FOR PARIS
The inside-out Pompidou Centre, named after former president of France Georges Pompidou, opened in Paris in 1977. Designed by Richard Rogers and Renzo Piano, the building has all its elevators, escalators, and utilities visible on the outside of the building.

•1975 SPACE LINK-UP
Closer collaboration between the USSR and the US extended to the space program when the US *Apollo 18* and the Soviet *Soyuz 19* docked while orbiting the Earth. The docking proved that two countries working together in space could produce results one alone could not.

Scales with a liquid crystal display

The rings of Uranus

•1977 RINGS OF URANUS
Scientists were surprised to discover in March 1977 that Uranus, like Saturn, was surrounded by a series of rings. The rings, 11 in all, are less than 6.2 miles (10 km) wide, and consist of boulders in orbit around the planet.

Punks in London

•1975 LIQUID CRYSTAL DISPLAYS
Liquid crystal molecules have a regular structure and are used for digital displays that require little power. By the mid-1970s, liquid crystal displays (LCDs) were in use in pocket calculators and some measuring instruments.

•1976 CONCORDE
The Anglo-French supersonic airliner *Concorde* first flew in 1969, but did not enter regular transatlantic service until 1976. Despite traveling at twice the speed of sound to cross the Atlantic Ocean in less than 3 hours, the noise and cost of the *Concorde* meant that only a few planes were produced. To date, the *Concorde* remains the only supersonic commercial aircraft in regular service.

Concorde

•1977 PUNKS
British youth rebelled in spectacular fashion during the punk movement. With spiky hair, safety-pin jewelry, and savage music, punks rejected traditional values when many in Britain were content to celebrate the Silver Jubilee of Queen Elizabeth's reign as monarch.

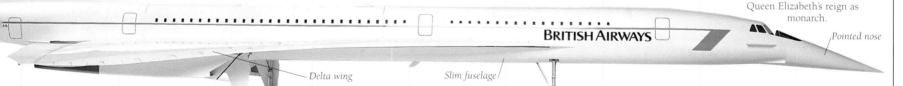

BRITISH AIRWAYS

Delta wing *Slim fuselage* *Pointed nose*

Juan Carlos II takes the throne as King of Spain

•1975 DEATH OF FRANCO
The death of the dictator General Franco, who had ruled Spain since 1939, was followed by the restoration of the Spanish monarchy. The new king, Juan Carlos II, paved the way for democratic elections, held in 1977.

•1976 SOWETO
In reaction to a proposal to make Afrikaans the compulsory language in school, black residents of Soweto township outside Johannesburg rioted in June 1976. At least 300 people were killed, and many thousand injured, when police opened fire on the demonstrators. The Soweto riots did much to alert the rest of the world to the harshness of the apartheid (separate development) regime of white-led South Africa.

•1976 LEBANON
The Middle Eastern state of Lebanon descended into civil war in 1975–76 when fighting broke out between Christians, Muslims, and Palestinian exiles. The capital, Beirut, was almost destroyed, prompting the armed intervention of neighboring Syria to restore peace.

Street fighting in Beirut

•1977 STEVE BIKO
Steve Biko was one of the leaders of the South African Black Consciousness movement, designed to give black South Africans pride in themselves and their history. In August 1977 he was arrested and interrogated for five days by South African police. He died in police custody, but despite evidence of police brutality, no one accepted responsibility for his death.

1978

| 1978 | 1979 | 1980 |

ARTS AND ENTERTAINMENT

•1978 DISCO
Disco – a mixture of rock, pop, and soul music aimed at the dance floor – became hugely popular in 1978 when *Saturday Night Fever* became the biggest-selling soundtrack album of all time. The film, starring John Travolta, was set in a discotheque in New York and features songs by the Bee Gees, including *Stayin' Alive*.

•1978 VIETNAM WAR FILMS
Five years after America withdrew from Vietnam, Hollywood began to examine the effects of the war. Both *Coming Home* and *The Deer Hunter* dealt with the experiences of individual soldiers after they returned from Vietnam.

•1979 ALIEN
Directed by Ridley Scott, *Alien* terrified movie audiences with its story of a violent alien monster lurking aboard the spacecraft *Nostromo*. The film starred Sigourney Weaver.

•1979 APOCALYPSE NOW
Directed by Francis Ford Coppola, *Apocalypse Now* presented another view of Vietnam. Starring Martin Sheen and Marlon Brando, the film depicts the dark side of the war.

Bjorn Borg

•1980 BJORN BORG
Swedish tennis player Bjorn Borg made tennis history in 1980 when he won the Wimbledon men's singles championship for the fifth successive time. This achievement was later eclipsed by the Czech-born player Martina Navratilova, who won the women's singles six times from 1982 through 1987.

•1980 JEAN-PAUL SARTRE
French philosopher Jean-Paul Sartre died at the age of 74. Sartre wrote novels and plays as well as philosophical works. All express his belief that the universe is meaningless and that people must take responsibility for their own actions.

SCIENCE AND DISCOVERY

Early desktop computer

Cassette deck

•1979 GAIA THEORY
British scientist James Lovelock proposed the Gaia theory – that the Earth is a single living organism, and that all life is linked together. He suggested that the Earth was therefore both self-regulating and self-organizing, just like any other organism, and thus could cope with temperature changes caused by the Greenhouse Effect.

James Lovelock

•1980 SMALLPOX ERADICATED
In May 1980 the World Health Organization announced that as a result of a worldwide vaccination program, the deadly smallpox virus had been completely eradicated. This was the first time that a disease had been conquered by mass vaccination.

Alphanumeric keyboard

EVERYDAY LIFE

•1978 PERSONAL COMPUTER
The world's first personal computer – the Altair 8800 – went on sale in 1975, but lacked both keyboard and screen and was sold only in kit form. In 1978 the personal computer revolution was born, when Apple and other firms launched computers that were ready to use, compact, cheap, and above all, user-friendly.

•1979 WALKMAN
In the Sony Corporation of Japan, executives were worried that their new product, a personal stereo with lightweight headphones, would not sell because it only played back pre-recorded cassettes. They were proved wrong when the Walkman became an instant success. Later models included a recording facility.

Walkman

•1979 OIL PRICE
The revolution in Iran and fears of conflict throughout the Middle East led to a doubling of oil prices in 1979. The effect was to increase price inflation throughout the world, contributing to an economic depression that would lead to mass unemployment throughout the early 1980s.

Volume control

Headphones

WORLD EVENTS

Mother Teresa

•1979 MOTHER TERESA
The Nobel Peace Prize was awarded to Mother Teresa, an Albanian nun who founded the Missionaries of Charity to work among the poor of Calcutta, in India. The Missionaries of Charity now operate schools, hospitals, and orphanages in more than 25 countries.

•1979 IRANIAN REVOLUTION
Islamic fundamentalist opposition to the rule of the pro-Western Shah of Iran forced the Shah to flee the country on January 16. Two weeks later Ayatollah Khomeini, exiled leader of Iran's Shia Moslems, returned from Paris to lead the country. He imposed a strict Islamic code and broke links with the US. The Iranian Revolution transformed the politics of the Middle East.

Iranian revolution

•1980 SOLIDARITY
Led by Lech Walesa, an electrician in the Gdansk shipyard, the independent Solidarity trade union was formed in Poland in August. Solidarity campaigned for better civil rights and higher wages, but was suppressed by the government. The union remained banned until 1989, when it was allowed to participate in free elections. One of its members then became the first non-Communist prime minister since the war. Walesa became president of Poland in 1990, a post he held for five years.

•1978 RED BRIGADE
In the late 1970s the terrorist Red Brigade conducted a violent campaign against the Italian state. On March 17 the brigade kidnapped the former prime minister, Aldo Moro, and held him hostage while they sought the release of their members held in prison. When the government refused to negotiate, Moro was killed and his body dumped in Rome.

1981

E.T. – the extraterrestrial

Michael Jackson

•1981 BOB MARLEY

Musician Bob Marley brought reggae music to the international stage with a string of famous songs, including *No Woman, No Cry* and *I Shot The Sheriff*. Marley used his music for a variety of political causes, including peace in his homeland of Jamaica. He died in Miami of cancer at the age of 36.

•1982 E.T.

Steven Spielberg's film of an extraterrestrial stranded on Earth was one of the most successful films of all time. It confirmed Spielberg, whose previous films included *Jaws* and *Close Encounters Of The Third Kind*, as Hollywood's leading director.

•1982 MICHAEL JACKSON

Michael Jackson, the former boy singer of the Jackson Five, became an international star with the release in 1982 of *Thriller*. The following year, it became the biggest-selling album of all time.

•1981 SPACE SHUTTLE

The world's first reusable spacecraft, the space shuttle *Columbia*, blasted off from Cape Kennedy on April 11. A space shuttle is launched by two solid-fuel booster rockets, which are jettisoned after takeoff for recovery and re-use. The shuttle itself then returns to land like a standard airplane.

•1982 COMPACT DISCS

Compact discs (CDs), which store sound digitally as a series of numbers, went on sale in 1982. During play, a laser beam scans the disc, reading the encoded sound and reproducing it clearly. By 1991 CDs had overtaken the sales of both records and cassette tapes.

•1983 STAR WARS

US president Ronald Reagan gave the go-ahead in March 1983 for an anti-ballistic missile (ABM) system that would destroy incoming missiles before they reached their target. This so-called "Star Wars" program involved constructing a defensive shield over the US using lasers, microwave beams, and other devices based both on land and in space.

NASA United States Columbia

Space shuttle

•1981 AIDS

The first official recognition that a deadly new disease existed came from officials at the Centers for Disease Control in the US in June 1981. Called AIDS (Acquired Immune Deficiency Syndrome), the disease attacks the body's natural defenses, leaving sufferers open to other infections and illnesses. In 1983, the probable cause of AIDS was identified as the Human Immunodeficiency Virus (HIV). Many thousands of people across the world have since died of the disease for which, as yet, there is no known cure.

Lens *LCD display*

Eyepiece

Camcorder

•1983 CAMCORDER

The development of the camcorder enabled amateur film makers to record pictures (and sometimes sound) on a video camera and play back the results on a television screen through a video cassette recorder. Home movies of family scenes became immensely popular.

•1982 UNEMPLOYMENT

In both Europe and America, inflation resulted in a worldwide economic recession and unemployment reached levels not seen since the 1930s.

Anwar Sadat

•1982 FALKLANDS WAR

On April 2 Argentinian troops occupied the Falkland Islands, a British dependency in the South Atlantic. Efforts to avert war failed, and in May British troops landed on the islands to expel the Argentinians. Nearly 1,000 people were killed before the Argentinians surrendered on June 14. Dispute between the two governments over ownership of the islands continues to this day.

•1982 ISRAEL INVADES LEBANON

Civil war and a lack of strong government allowed Palestinian groups to use Lebanon as a base from which to attack Israel. In June 1982 Israel launched a full-scale invasion of Lebanon to drive the Palestinians out, which they achieved by the end of August.

Argentine prisoners, 1982

British army survival kit

•1981 SADAT KILLED

The Egyptian president Anwar Sadat was assassinated in October by Islamic extremists angry at his policy of peace with Israel. In 1977 Sadat had visited Jerusalem, beginning talks that led to a peace treaty the following year between Egypt and Israel – the first time a neighboring Arab country had recognized Israel's right to exist. Sadat and the Israeli leader Menachem Begin shared the 1978 Nobel Peace Prize.

•1983 BEIRUT BOMBS

During 1982, US, French, and Italian peacekeeping forces had arrived in Beirut, capital of Lebanon. On October 23 1983, in two suicide bomb attacks, Muslim extremists drove trucks containing explosives into the US and French military headquarters. In total, 241 US Marines and 58 French paratroopers were killed.

1984

ARTS AND ENTERTAINMENT

•1984 MINIMALIST MUSIC

In reaction to the abstraction of much modern music, American composers such as Terry Riley, Steve Reich, and Philip Glass developed a new kind of music often called minimalist. These composers use hypnotically repeating rhythms and simple harmonies to build up layers of sounds that change imperceptibly.

Hong Kong and Shanghai Bank building

•1985 HONG KONG AND SHANGHAI BANK BUILDING

Completed at an estimated cost of $750 million, the headquarters of the Hong Kong and Shanghai Bank in Hong Kong is one of the most sophisticated buildings ever constructed. The building, designed by British architect Norman Foster, hangs on eight steel masts, creating huge clear spaces inside.

•1985 LIVE AID

In response to the Ethiopian famine of the early 1980s, Irish rock star Bob Geldof organized two simultaneous live concerts in London and Philadelphia to raise money for the starving. The concerts were watched on television by 1.5 billion people in 160 countries.

Live Aid, 1985

•1986 *PHANTOM OF THE OPERA*

Composer of musicals Andrew Lloyd Webber had his first success with *Joseph And The Amazing Technicolor Dreamcoat* in 1968. A string of successes over the next 25 years, including *Cats* (1981) and *Phantom Of The Opera* (1986), made Lloyd Webber the most successful popular composer of his day.

SCIENCE AND DISCOVERY

•1984 DNA

Everyone has their own unique pattern of DNA, present in every cell in our bodies. British geneticist Alex Jeffreys suggested that it would be possible to use the DNA patterns just like fingerprints for identification purposes. Suspected criminals can now be identified by the DNA in any blood or saliva left at the scene of a crime.

A DNA "fingerprint"

•1985 ATOM SMASHER

The world's largest atom smasher opened in Illinois on October 13. The device, known as an accelerator, measures 4 miles (6.4 km) in diameter. It uses a series of huge magnets to fire particles, such as electrons, at great speed into other particles in order to break them up into smaller subatomic particles. The collisions that take place enable physicists to study the structure of matter.

False-color image of Halley's Comet

•1986 COMET VISIT

Halley's Comet, named after the 18th-century British astronomer Edmond Halley, paid its regular 76-year visit to Earth during 1986. The space probe *Giotto* was sent up to intercept the comet, flying within 600 miles (960 km) of it. *Giotto* took samples of the vapor in its gaseous tail, and discovered that the comet's nucleus was in fact a jagged lump of dirt and ice measuring 10 x 5 miles (16 x 8 km).

EVERYDAY LIFE

•1984 ENVIRONMENT

Concerns about industrial pollution and the effect of heavy industry on the environment rose sharply during the 1980s. A leak from a chemical factory's storage tank killed at least 2,000 people in the Indian city of Bhopal in December 1984 – one of the worst environmental disasters of recent years.

•1985 MOBILE TELEPHONES

The image that summed up the go-getting, get-rich-quick attitude of the 1980s was the mobile telephone. Linked to a series of low-powered radio stations, the mobile telephone enabled its user to make a call at any time or place, even from a moving car. Different frequencies were used to avoid interference between phones.

Antenna

Loudspeaker

Mobile telephone

Microphone

Mikhail Gorbachov

•1986 CHERNOBYL

In April, there was an explosion at the Chernobyl nuclear power plant in what is now Ukraine. The explosion caused an international environmental alert as radioactive clouds drifted westward across eastern Europe, Britain, and Scandinavia. The region surrounding Chernobyl was evacuated immediately after the explosion but, despite this precaution, many people were affected by radioactivity. The Chernobyl accident renewed doubts about the safety and efficiency of nuclear power.

Washing radioactive material from a vehicle on the outskirts of Chernobyl

WORLD EVENTS

•1984 MRS. GANDHI KILLED

India's prime minister Indira Gandhi was assassinated on October 31 by one of her Sikh bodyguards. Sikh extremists demanded independence within India for the Sikh homeland of the Punjab, and conducted a violent campaign throughout the 1980s. Mrs. Gandhi was succeeded by her son Rajiv.

•1985 GORBACHEV

Mikhail Gorbachev became the Soviet leader in March, promising *perestroika* (reconstruction) of the Soviet state, and a policy of *glasnost* (openness) to give greater freedom to the Russian people. He also tried to improve relations between the USSR and the US.

•1985 GREENPEACE SHIP SUNK

On July 11, French secret agents sank the Greenpeace ship *Rainbow Warrior* in Auckland Harbour, New Zealand, to prevent its crew from protesting against French nuclear tests in the South Pacific. Led by New Zealand, a group of South Pacific nations later signed the Treaty of Rarotonga, creating a nuclear-free zone in the region.

•1986 HAITI

In February "Baby Doc" – Jean-Claude Duvalier, the hated dictator of Haiti and son of the infamous "Papa Doc" – was forced into exile by an army coup. The Duvaliers had ruled the country between them since 1957.

•1986 THE PHILIPPINES

Popular discontent with the long-running dictatorial rule of President Ferdinand Marcos of the Philippines led to his being overthrown in February 1986. He was succeeded by Corazón Aquino, widow of a former opposition leader.

1987

1987

1989

•1987 WARHOL

Andy Warhol, a member of the Pop Art movement in New York, died in February. He began work as a commercial illustrator, but achieved lasting fame for his silk-screen portraits of stars such as Marilyn Monroe and Elvis Presley. Warhol also painted Pop Art images of consumer goods such as soup cans and cola bottles. Through his studio, the Factory in New York, he made films and produced rock bands, most notably the Velvet Underground.

Andy Warhol

•1988 STOCKHAUSEN

The completion of the opera *Montag* (Monday) by German composer Karlheinz Stockhausen marked the latest stage in an ambitious plan to write an opera for every day of the week. When completed sometime during the 21st century, the cycle of seven operas, entitled *Licht* (light), will be one of the most adventurous pieces of music ever written.

•1989 BATMAN MOVIE

With Jack Nicholson as the Joker and Michael Keaton as the hero, the Batman television series finally came to the big screen in 1989. A soundtrack by rock singer Prince accompanied the action in Gotham City. The same cast reappeared in *Batman Returns* in 1992, with a new cast headed by Val Kilmer starring in the 1995 version *Batman Forever*.

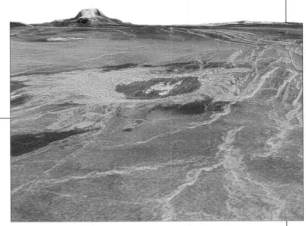

The surface of Venus as seen by *Magellan*

•1987 SUPERNOVA

The first supernova since 1604 that could be seen with the naked eye was discovered on February 24. Supernova 1987A was seen in the Large Magellanic Cloud, the nearest galaxy to our own Milky Way. Even at a distance of 170,000 light-years, the supernova lit up the night sky for two weeks. A supernova occurs when a massive star collapses at the end of its life. The core may survive to become a small pulsating neutron star (pulsar) or even a black hole.

Stephen Hawking

•1988 HAWKING

British physicist Stephen Hawking achieved international success with his book *A Brief History of Time*. In it he investigated what might have happened in the first few moments of the Big Bang that created the Universe, proposing that there is no beginning and no end to time. Hawking's achievements are all the more remarkable because he suffers from motor neurone disease and is unable to communicate except through a computer.

•1989 *MAGELLAN* PROBE

Put together with spare parts from previous space missions, the US *Magellan* probe was launched toward Venus on May 4. *Magellan* orbits Venus every 3 hr 9 min, using radar to map most of the planet over 243 days (one Venus day). By analyzing the data on Earth, scientists can build up a picture of the planet.

•1987 FAX MACHINE

The first patent to send images down a telegraph wire was taken out by Scotsman Alexander Bain in 1843. Newspaper offices later used complex machines with a rotating drum to send pictures around the world, but it wasn't until the mid-1980s that fax machines became small enough for office and home use. The modern fax (or facsimile) machine uses a microprocessor to convert words and pictures into a code that can be sent quickly and reliably down a telephone wire.

Buttons for dialling

Telephone handset

Fax machine

Tray for fax messages

•1989 IVORY BAN

At the close of the 1980s elephants and rhinoceroses faced extinction at the hands of hunters who killed them for their tusks and horns. In response to worldwide protests, the Convention on International Trade in Endangered Species (CITES) imposed a worldwide ban on trading in ivory. To show support for the ban, a number of countries made bonfires of elephant tusks.

Burning ivory

•1987 SINGLE EUROPEAN ACT

The European Community (EC) of 12 nations took a huge stride toward European unity when the Single European Act came into force in 1987. The act increased the powers of the multinational European Parliament and set a target date of the end of 1992 for a free and unified market of goods and services throughout the EC.

Benazir Bhutto

•1988 BENAZIR BHUTTO

Benazir Bhutto, daughter of the Pakistan prime minister Zulfiqar Ali Bhutto, went into exile when her father was executed for treason in 1979. She returned to Pakistan in 1986, and led her father's Pakistan People's Party to victory in the general elections of 1988.

•1988 IRAN-IRAQ WAR ENDS

After eight years of bloody fighting, the war between Iran and Iraq finally came to an end when both sides agreed to a ceasefire on August 20. The war began in 1980 when Iraq tried to capture a strategic waterway at the head of the Persian Gulf. It soon developed into trench warfare along the length of the border as neither side had the capacity necessary for a decisive victory. Many hundreds of thousands of people were killed, many by chemical weapons such as mustard gas.

•1989 BERLIN WALL

Faced with a mass exodus of its people through Hungary into West Germany, the East German government pulled down the wall that separated East from West Berlin. The fall of the wall symbolized the mood of rapid change that was sweeping across Eastern Europe as the USSR relaxed its grip on the area.

•1989 TIANANMEN SQUARE

The Chinese government cracked down on pro-democracy protesters in Tiananmen Square in Beijing by sending in tanks and armed troops. Hundreds of people were killed, and many more reformers imprisoned throughout China.

1990–2000 The final decade

The revolution that began with Mikhail Gorbachev taking power in Russia in 1985 and ended with the collapse of the USSR in 1991 turned the world upside down. The old divided world in which capitalist America faced Communist Russia came to an abrupt end, leaving in its place a new order with the US as the unchallenged leader of the world. Russia and the newly independent states of eastern Europe all held democratic elections and turned toward the US and western Europe for advice and help in transforming their economies from state control to private enterprise.

US astronaut working near the space shuttle

An uncertain future

But the transition from Communism to capitalism has not been easy for many countries. Failure to deliver economic prosperity made many of the newly democratic governments in Russia and eastern Europe quickly become unpopular, allowing the former Communist parties to return to power. In addition, the damage caused by old, inefficient industries and a stockpile of aging nuclear weapons has left many countries with environmental problems that will be hard to overcome.

Statues of Lenin and other Communist leaders were removed from many cities

SPACE EXPLORATION

Throughout the 1990s, the emphasis in space exploration has shifted from headline-grabbing human voyages to exclusively scientific research aimed at finding out about our nearest neighbors in space. Probes launched during the 1970s and 1980s continue to send back information as they travel toward the outer reaches of the Solar System, while *Ulysses*, launched in 1990, headed in a huge loop via Jupiter to explore the poles of the Sun in 1994–95. The *Hubble Space Telescope*, also launched in 1990, enables astronomers to get a better view of space far above the distorting atmosphere of the Earth.

High-gain antenna

Primary mirror housing

Solar panel

Handrail for astronauts

Equipment storage

TOWARD THE MILLENNIUM: 1990–2000

SOVIET COLLAPSE

By the time the USSR collapsed in December 1991, world communism was dead. Only North Korea continued as if nothing had happened. China and Vietnam began to modernize their economies by allowing limited private enterprise, and the Cuban government relaxed its strong control over its economy. But in Russia the transition from Communism to capitalism has been far from smooth.

President of the Russian Confederation, Boris Yeltsin

THE GULF WAR

The invasion of Kuwait in February 1991 to free it from Iraqi occupation was the most technologically advanced war every fought. State-of-the-art weaponry, including map-reading missiles and smart bombs able to pinpoint precise targets bombarded the Iraqi capital of Baghdad. Millions of people watched the conflict unfold as it was broadcast live on international television.

US infantryman in the camouflage uniform worn during the Gulf War

US stealth aircraft bombed Iraq

AN AGING POPULATION

As a result of rising living standards around the world and better standards of health care and nutrition, the average life expectancy for men is expected to rise from 62 in 1990 to more than 70 in 2020. Women can expect to live to an average age of 75 by the same year. But because the birth rate is falling as people worldwide decide to have smaller families, the average population of the world is becoming older and older.

The Pacific region

One part of the world largely unaffected by these momentous changes has been eastern Asia. Japan and the four "little dragons" of South Korea, Taiwan, Hong Kong, and Singapore have been among the most successful economies in the world in recent years. Together they have made the Pacific Rim (the countries surrounding the Pacific Ocean, including the US and Canada) the fastest expanding trade area in the world. As the importance of the Pacific Rim grows, so the relative importance of Europe continues to decline. Even the one remaining Communist power in the world, China, has begun to modernize its economy. With its huge population and vast natural resources, it is on the way to becoming the industrial giant of the next century.

Aperture door

Light shield

Hubble Space Telescope

The world in 2000

As the world approaches the next millennium, industrial growth is having a serious impact on the planet's environment. The Greenhouse Effect, caused by pollution, is slowly raising average temperatures around the world. Scarce resources, such as water and wood, are being used up faster than nature can produce them, and supplies of oil and natural gas are slowly running out.

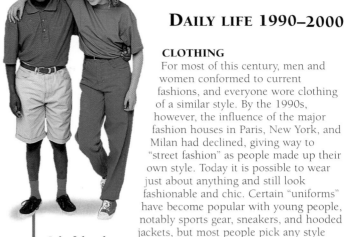

Colorful and comfortable children's clothing, 1990s

DAILY LIFE 1990–2000

CLOTHING
For most of this century, men and women conformed to current fashions, and everyone wore clothing of a similar style. By the 1990s, however, the influence of the major fashion houses in Paris, New York, and Milan had declined, giving way to "street fashion" as people made up their own style. Today it is possible to wear just about anything and still look fashionable and chic. Certain "uniforms" have become popular with young people, notably sports gear, sneakers, and hooded jackets, but most people pick any style that they are happy with. Fashions from previous decades, especially the 1960s and 1970s, have been revived, and ethnic clothes are popular.

ELECTRONICS
The electronic revolution of the past 20 years has transformed people's lives in the 1990s. New forms of entertainment, such as satellite and cable TV, are now relayed to every house, and more and more people are working from home, linked to an office by computer and modem. The Internet now allows people to access information held in libraries on the other side of the world, as well as to hold digital conversations with millions of unseen subscribers around the planet. Marshall McLuhan's 1962 vision of an electronic "global village" has now become a reality.

Male and female clothing, 1990s

COMPUTERS
Computer technology is continuing to develop at breathtaking speed, with faster processors powering increasingly versatile computers. Computer scientists are now working on voice recognition systems that will enable a computer to recognize vocal instructions rather than rely on manual commands received letter by letter through the keyboard.

SOUTH AFRICA
The election in 1994 of a multi-racial democratic government in South Africa led by Nelson Mandela inspired the world to hope that if peace and reconciliation between different peoples could occur in South Africa, it could happen elsewhere, too.

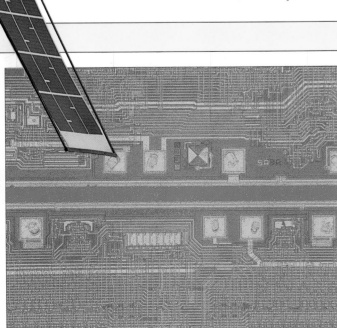

Computer circuitry on a microchip

Nelson Mandela votes in the South African election

Rain forest destruction

ENVIRONMENTAL CONCERNS
The UN Conference on Environment and Development, held in Rio de Janeiro in June 1992, recognized the importance of protecting the world's environment in the face of constant attack from industrial and economic growth. However, translating those hopes for a greener future into reality remains a problem, because many poor nations wish to develop their industries.

1990

ARTS AND ENTERTAINMENT

A "screen" from a CD-ROM

•1990 THREE TENORS
Three of the world's finest operatic tenors – Placido Domingo, Jose Carreras, and Luciano Pavarotti – sang in an open-air concert to celebrate the World Cup taking place in Italy. A version of Puccini's *Nessun Dorma* propelled opera to heights of popularity usually enjoyed only by rock music.

•1991 CD-ROM
Compact discs opened up a multitude of new educational and entertainment opportunities in the 1990s. A CD-ROM (read-only memory) can hold an entire encyclopedia, presenting the information as text, graphics, video clips, photographs, and sound.

Jurassic Park film still

•1992 JURASSIC PARK
Steven Spielberg's run of hugely popular films continued with *Jurassic Park*. Based on the novel by Michael Crichton, the film tells the story of a wealthy businessman who stocked an amusement park with genetically engineered dinosaurs.

•1995 DAMIEN HIRST
British artist Damien Hirst attracted widespread criticism with his exhibits of dead sheep and cows. Hirst was awarded the Turner Prize for art in 1995.

SCIENCE AND DISCOVERY

The asteroid Gaspra

•1991 ASTEROID GASPRA
The US space probe *Galileo* took the first high-quality photographs of an asteroid when it flew through the asteroid belt between Mars and Jupiter. Pictures of the asteroid Gaspra – a large lump of rock – were sent back to Earth in October.

•1993 BIOSPHERE II
On September 27, a team of eight researchers breathed fresh air for the first time in two years. They had been sealed inside an artificial environment, Biosphere II, in Arizona. Biosphere II resembled a large greenhouse, and contained small-scale versions of typical Earth habitats.

Stars form in the clouds of the Eagle nebula

•1995 STAR FORMATION
The *Hubble Space Telescope* sent back high-quality images of the Eagle nebula, showing star formation. The nebula, a huge cloud of gas and dust, is located about 7,000 light-years from Earth. Within the cloud, scientists can see clumps of protostars, an early stage in stars' evolution. Some of the protostars are surrounded by an outer shell of cooler material that may later form planetary systems.

EVERYDAY LIFE

•1990 WORLD POPULATION
The world's population passed 5 billion for the first time in the 1980s, reaching 5.295 billion by 1990. More than half this total lived in towns and cities.

•1990 PORTABLE COMPUTERS
The development of portable "laptop" and "notebook" computers enabled users to work on board a train or an aircraft. Portable computers have LCD (liquid crystal) screens and are powered by rechargeable batteries.

"Notebook" computer

•1994 TOURISM
With increasing numbers of people seeking vacations "away from it all," the harmful effects of tourism became evident during the 1990s. In many poorer countries, the main source of income is tourism. However, the vast numbers of people wishing to visit such wonders as the Great Barrier Reef and the Galapagos Islands are having a negative effect on the local environment.

Tourists in London

WORLD EVENTS

Smoke-filled skies over
Kuwait, 1991

US M16A1 rifle
with M203
grenade launcher

•1991 GULF WAR
Anxious to extend its influence in the region and to grab additional oil reserves, Iraq invaded neighboring Kuwait in August 1990. After the invasion was condemned by the UN, a bombing campaign against Iraq was followed by a 100-hour land war. In February 1991, Kuwait was liberated by an international coalition headed by the US.

•1991-92 BREAKUP OF USSR
A failing economy, food shortages, and agitation for independence combined to weaken Mikhail Gorbachev's power in the USSR. In 1991 most republics declared independence, and Gorbachev resigned as president on December 25.

•1993 PLO-ISRAEL AGREEMENT
Israel and the PLO signed a peace treaty in Washington on September 13. The treaty allowed for eventual Palestinian self-rule in the Gaza Strip and the West Bank.

•1994 ANC WINS ELECTIONS
Freed in 1990 after 26 years in jail, Nelson Mandela negotiated a new multiracial constitution for South Africa. In April 1994 he led the ANC party to victory in the first democratic elections, becoming the first black president of South Africa.

War graves in former Yugoslavia

•1991-95 FORMER YUGOSLAVIA
Tension between the six republics of Yugoslavia led to the collapse of the country in June 1991. Slovenia, Croatia, and Bosnia declared their independence, but were opposed by Serbia. For the next four years, war raged in Croatia and Bosnia as Serbs fought to establish a greater Serbia by "ethnically cleansing" the region of all non-Serbs.

Future Trends

VIRTUAL REALITY

Virtual reality (VR) became reality in the mid-1990s when powerful computers created realistic three-dimensional scenes. Viewed either through goggles, or directly onscreen, virtual reality systems allow the user to move through a French cathedral, for example, like a bird flying through the building itself.

COMPUTERIZED ACTORS

Once dismissed as mere special effects, computer-generated images will soon be able to replace human film actors. Improved technology will result in films being made entirely by computer.

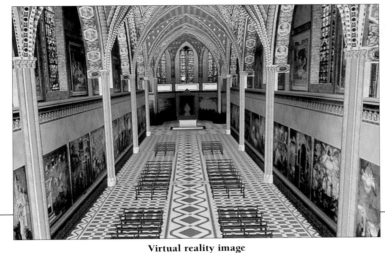

Virtual reality image

MOVIES BY PHONE

No longer will it be necessary to visit your local theater or rent a video to see your favorite movie. Soon, entire movie libraries will be available through the phone line. Once you have selected the movie, your choice will be relayed down a phone line to your domestic television.

NON-HUMAN MUSIC

The music you listen to in the future may well be written entirely by machine. Whatever musical style you like, there will be a computer program that can assemble electronic sounds into a suitable piece of music.

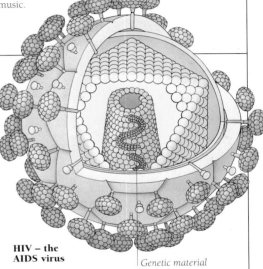

HIV – the AIDS virus

Genetic material

GENOME PROJECT

In 1988, US scientists established the Human Genome Organization (HUGO) in Washington, DC, to compile a complete computer "map" of the human genetic system. When the map is complete sometime early in the next century, geneticists hope that they will be able to cure all known genetic diseases – those which are passed on from parents to children.

AIDS RESEARCH

Although most scientists are now convinced that the Human Immunodeficiency Virus (HIV) is the cause of AIDS, they are no nearer finding either a prevention or a cure. Scientists are working to inhibit or slow down the reproduction of HIV and prevent it from infecting new cells. In this way they hope to neutralize the virus.

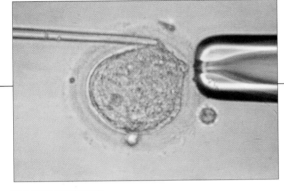

Removing material from a human egg for genetic research

Working from home

SMART HOUSES

The average home currently contains 145 microprocessors in electronic items ranging from televisions and stereos to heating thermostats and toasters. At the moment, there is no universal computer language enabling these processors to communicate with each other. Scientists are currently working on a network to link these devices together, so the user can monitor and control everything via a single computer or television screen.

WORKING FROM HOME

As more and more people choose to work from home, new ways of linking home workers together are being devised. Modems to relay information down phone lines by computer plus video phones to connect people around the world will soon signal the end of the traditional office.

FUTURE CARS

Concern over vehicle exhaust pollution and the future scarcity of fuel is leading scientists to develop zero-emission vehicles. These new cars will run on sophisticated batteries that take some of their power from the sun.

Concept design for a future car

INTERNET

Originally set up in 1969 to link military computers together in a common network, the Internet grew rapidly in the 1980s as more and more civilian users joined. Today more than 10 million computers are linked in a worldwide information network. In the future, people will turn to the Internet for information the way previous generations consulted books.

Internet connections

SUPER CITY

Within a decade, a city of 40 million people will have risen up just north of Hong Kong. The new city has no name at present, but will become the largest in the world with a population greater than most European states.

OZONE HOLE

Scientists remain unsure about the precise effect of burning fossil fuels on the environment, although everyone accepts that the Greenhouse Effect is raising world temperatures. According to some forecasts, the rising temperatures could lead to the polar ice caps melting, which would cause flooding in many low-lying countries.

Index

Pop-up toaster, 1930s

Bristol fighter, 1917

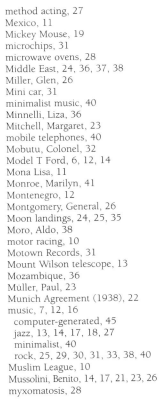

Tape recorder, 1950s

Acknowledgments

The publisher would like to thank the following for their kind permission to reproduce the following photographs:

Key: l=left r=right c=centre t=top b=bottom or below a= above
Picture Credits
Advertising Archives: 14br; Allsport: 38tr; Arcaid: 16tl, 21tr, 29tr; Bridgeman Art Library / City of Bristol Museum & Art Gallery: 9tr; / Fine Art Society, London: 11tl; /Imperial War Museum: 13tc; /Trustees of the V&A: 9b; Andrew Cormack: 33bc; Peter Clayton: 17cc; Corbis: 7bcl; /Bettman: 18tc, 20bl, 21tl, 21cl, 21bl, 22tl, 23tr, 23bl, 24bl, 27bc, 30bl, 32br, 33bl;/ Bettman / Underwood: 13tl; / Bettman / UPI: 14tr, 22bl, 23cl, 23cc,26tr, 26br, 27tr, 27tc, 28br, 29tl, 29bc, 30cc, 30br, 31bc, 31br, 40bl; Mary Evans Picture Library: 7bl; Frank Spooner / Gamma`:` Michel Laurent 36bl, Catherine Leroy 37br, Shone 40br, 38br; Bob Gathaway: 42/43c; Glasgow Museums: 18cc; Ronald Grant Archive: 23tl, 31tl, 32tr, 37tl, 39tl; Hulton Getty Picture Collection: 9tl, 9bcl, 10cl, 11tc, 13bl, 16bl, 17cr, 19cc, 20tl, 26ccb, 26bl, 27bl, 30cl, 31bl; London Transport Museum: 8cr; Lee Miller Archive: 7bc; Magnum / Abbas: 36tc; Liz McAulay: 34cl; Museum of Moving Image: 2tr; Nasa: 17tcr, 24tl, 35cc, 37tr, 39cl, 41tr, 42tc, 44cl; National Army Museum: 14bl, 24bcl; National Maritime Museum: 6bc, 24-25, 35br; Noordwijk Space Expo: 25bl; Robert Opie Collection: 17cc, 20cl; Popperfoto: 6tl, 6tr, 8tcl, 8bl, 8br, 10bc, 11cbr, 11bl, 12bl, 13br, 14tl, 15bcl, 16cc, 16bc, 17tl, 18tr, 18bl, 18br, 19bl, 19br, 20tcl, 20br, 21cr, 21br, 22bc, 22br, 26cr, 28bl, 29cc, 31tr, 32bl, 33tc, 33br, 35bl, 36tr, 37cr, 39br, 42cl, 42br; Rex Features: 42br; 8tcr, 11tr, 12br, 16tr, 17bl, 19tl, 26tl, 32tl, 33tl, 33cc, 34br, 35tc, 36br, 39br, 40tr, 41cl, 41br, 43bc, 44tr, 44cl, 45br; /AOCRD 7tl, / Nils Jorgenson 40l, /David Lomax 38cr, / Action Press 44br, /ITN: 38bl; / Sipa press: Eva Rudling 41tl,, Bob Strong 41bl, 23br,

28bl, 30tl, 34tl, 37bl, 39bl,; / The Times; 44cr; Science Museum, London: 8bcl, 18bcl, 20tcr; Science Photo Library: / Gregory Dimijian 43 br, / Simon Fraser 25tl, 34cr, / James King Holmes 45cl, / Mehau Kulyk 45bl, / Andrew Mc Clenaghan 19tcl, / Peter Menzel 44bl./ NASA 27tl, / Space Telescope Science Institute/ NASA 44cr./ David Parker 43bl, / Plailly/ Eurelios 45tc./ Royal Observatory, Edinburgh 40cr, / Sheila Terry 45cc; Smithsonian Institution: 10tl, 17tcl, 22tr; Sony: 5b; Trustees of the Tate Gallery, London: Umberto Boccioni, 'Unique Forms of Continuity in Space' 12tl, / Mark Rothko, 'Untitled', ARS, NY and DACS, London 1996 28tr / Roy Lichtenstein, 'Whaam!', Roy Lichtenstein / DACS 1996 30tr.

Every effort has been made to trace the copyright holders. Dorling Kindersley apologises for any unintentional omissions and would be pleased, in such cases, to add an acknowledgement in future editions.

Early gramophone